Naughties
Nudies & Bathing Beauties

by Sharon Hope Weintraub

Published by  Hobby House Press, Inc.
Cumberland, Maryland 21502

Dedication

This book is dedicated to my mother, who started my collection with my first "naughtie" twenty years ago and has continued to aid and abet me ever since.

Acknowledgments

I must thank all my fellow collectors who have shared their collections and knowledge with me, with special gratitude to Dr. Rex Bonnstetter for his enjoyable correspondence, exceptional generosity in exchanging information and photographs, and allowing me to visit his collection. I must also thank my brother, David, who patiently and over long distance helped me tame a sometimes recalcitrant personal computer.

Special thanks and acknowledgment go to Mr. Monty Moncrief, from whose talented hands and camera came the beautiful photographs of my collection. He spent many hours in the hot Houston sunshine making sure his tiny models were seen only at their best.

Front Cover: Two bisque figurines consisting of three bathing beauties with their original silk net bathing suits and mohair wigs. Both figurines are described in more detail in the chapter "Crowning Glory" as *Illustrations CG1* and *CG4*.

Title Page: 8in (20cm) tall bisque figurine by Goebel. *See page 72, Illustration G11, for further information.*

Back Cover: (Left) 5in (13cm) long bisque figurine by Goebel. *See page 70, Illustration G8, for further information.*
(Right) 6¼in (16cm) tall bisque figurine by Schafer and Vater. *See page 81, Illustration SV10, for further information.*

Naughties, Nudies and Bathing Beauties is an independent study by the author, Sharon Hope Weintraub, and published by Hobby House Press, Inc. The research and publication of this book were not sponsored in any way by the manufacturers of the dolls, doll costumes, doll accessories and other related collectibles featured in this study. Photographs of the collectibles were from the collection of Sharon Hope Weintraub at the time the photo was taken unless otherwise credited with the caption.

The values given within this book are intended as value guides rather than fixed prices. The values quoted are as accurate as possible but in the case of errors, typographical, clerical or otherwise, the author and publisher assume no liability or responsibility for any loss incurred by users of this book.

Additional copies of this book may be purchased at $12.95
from
HOBBY HOUSE PRESS, INC.
900 Frederick Street
Cumberland, Maryland 21502
or from your favorite bookstore or dealer.
Please add $4.75 per copy for postage.

Table of Contents

Introductions and Definitions

Sometime during forays into antique shows and flea markets, most antiquers have come across a bisque or china novelty that the dealer labeled a bathing beauty or naughtie. The item may have been a figurine of a lovely lady in painted swimsuit, or one of real lace, or none at all. Perhaps it was a dainty damsel in molded dishabille, or a figurine that seemed to be a seated maiden in demure dress, only to reveal that when she was turned over she had neglected to fasten her knickers. Or it might have been a hollow figurine of a little boy answering nature's call or a woman cupping her breasts with a hole (or holes) placed in the appropriate orifice(s). Sometimes the item came with a story it was a French figurine copied from a naughty postcard or a rare Victorian item. The seller might assert the object was specially made as a souvenir for brothel patrons or, in the case of the hollow figurines, was a perfume bottle. Many of these amusing knick-knacks have found their way into curio cabinets, and sometimes into collections of the same genre, but search as he or she might, the collector finds little in reference material or information.

This book will give the curious and the collector some idea as to what these little objects were, who made them, and when they were made. In writing this book, I was forced to debunk a few myths, which should not devalue these delightful collectibles. The majority of these figurines, if not all, are of German, not French, manufacture. While some might date before the turn of the century, many were produced when Edward VII, not Victoria, sat on the English throne, and large numbers were made into the 1930s. Well known manufacturers displayed these items in their catalogues along side doll heads and utilitarian pincushion dolls, and they were made in such numbers that it is doubtful these risqué bisque and china objects were meant to be bought in brothels (nor is it likely a customer of such an establishment would care to publicize his patronage with a souvenir). They do not seem to have been specifically sold for perfume bottles, and many are made in such a way that they would have been unsuitable receptacles for expensive scents. Evidence suggests that they were merely mass produced novelties created by German manufacturers in hopes of coaxing money out of the pockets of a population rejecting the restrictions of Victorian society, yet often these curiosities display amazing workmanship and imagination. They were made in such numbers and variety that no book could contain them all, but I have tried to include examples of the various types, and to group them in a way to ease reference for the reader. There seems to be no set glossary for these collectibles, but I have used the following definitions throughout the book:

Bathing Beauty: A bisque or china figurine of a woman either wearing a painted bathing suit, a bathing suit of real material, or nude but meant to be sold in a bathing suit of net or lace. The last type usually have solid dome heads that were covered by mohair wigs and bathing caps, wear molded one strap or ballet type bathing slippers, and are in a pose that would have made dressing possible (ie: the thighs are not molded together and there is no object, such as a book or lute, molded to the torso). Usually these figures have no base.

Flipper: A bisque or china figurine that appears to be simply an innocent knick-knack which, when turned over, exposes an erotic view. The most common examples are of seated women with their full skirts flowing around them, but revealing bare bottoms underneath.

Mermaid: A bisque or china figurine whose upper half is of a woman, but whose lower portion is a single or double fish tail. Usually there is no base.

Naughtie: Generally, a bisque or china figurine of a woman wearing molded undergarments. Usually there is no base. In a broader sense, naughtie can be used for the entire genre of flippers, nudies, and squirters.

Nudie: A bisque or china figurine of a nude woman, usually without a base, who, due to her pose or history, was apparently intended to be sold au naturel.

Sea Nymph: A bisque or china figurine of a woman, not a mermaid or bathing beauty, posing in or on a sea shell, turtle shell, or other item of an aquatic theme.

Squirter: A small hollow bisque or china figurine with a large opening on top and one or two smaller holes worked into the design. The most common type is a little boy urinating, with the small hole between his legs. Less common variations are of a woman holding her breasts with openings in one or both breasts or with an opening between her legs. Originally, some, if not all, of these figures, were sold with a rubber bulb, similar to that found on an eyedropper, fastened over the large hole. When the object was filled with water and the bulb squeezed, water would squirt out of the smaller opening or openings.

Manufacture and Manufacturers

The most persistent story about naughties, nudies, and bathing beauties is that they are of French origin, though most, if not all, actually were manufactured in Germany. This seems to be based on two preconceptions. One is the stereotyped view of the French as a chic, sophisticated race with joie de vivre who originated such naughty delights as the can-can, the Folies, and risqué postcards, while the Germans are categorized as solid, stolid people with practical bourgeois tastes. Like all such stereotypes, these are unfair and untrue. Berlin of the 1920s could match even the steamiest, and seamiest, shows of France and many of those "French" postcards rolled off of German presses. The second preconception comes from the earliest days of doll collecting when the finest dolls were categorized as French, while the Germans were credited only with the vapid legions of dull, dolly-faced dolls that forced the more exquisite French products off the market by sheer mass produced numbers. Research has shown that not only were the French capable of creating some very inferior products, some of those pale, luminous heads on proudly displayed bebes came from the kilns of such German makers as Simon and Halbig, who produced products for the French market. There is no doubt the bathing beauties and their risqué kin in this book claim Germany as their birthplace. Almost all German doll manufacturers of any size advertised these figurines along side their dolls, pincushion dolls, and knick-knacks. Kestner and Galluba and Hofmann proudly displayed these wares in their catalogues, and the marks of William Goebel and Schafer and Vater are sometimes found on the loveliest of ladies. Their German origin should not disgrace or denigrate these works because the German manufacturers were capable of producing some of the finest bisque and china pieces in the world. However, the old prejudices still linger. For example, one well meaning dealer once offered me, as French, a roguish eyed lady clad only in white chemise and black stockings that she had been told was purchased in Paris as a souvenir during World War I by a soldier for his sweetheart, even though the figurine bore the mark of Schafer and Vater. The little figurine might have called Paris home at one time, but her birthplace was clearly Germany.

While collectors may think of the products of these German companies as delightful, their makers were business people and saw these items, like their dolls and other products, as money makers. The bisque and china industry in Germany was big business, not only because of the size of its output, but also the cost of the industry as well. Huge kilns, and costly coal to fuel these kilns, were needed to produce enough products to make the factories profitable. Plaster of Paris molds had to be made and constantly replaced as they wore out. Workers were needed to sculpt, cast, assemble, fire, and decorate the products, and although the pay and factory conditions for these men, women, and children were abysmal by our modern standards, thousands were employed in the industry. Although some early doll books romanticize German bisque and china doll production as a cottage industry, research has established that to produce the huge quantity, and often high quality, of bisque and china dolls and related items, this was an enormous and highly developed industry requiring extensive investment and resources to be profitable and productive. The many steps, and hands, necessary to produce a single figurine could only be supplied by such factories.

First, a prototype for the figurine had to be sculpted. The extraordinary artistry of many of the bathing beauties, naughties, and nudies in this book show the German manufacturers often employed skilled sculptors and artists. Once the prototype had been made (and no doubt carefully scrutinized as to both artistic and commercial appeal by the factory manager), another artist, the mold maker, took over. Making a mold is much more than arbitrarily casting the prototype in a piece of plaster, then cutting the mold in half. In making a mold of the prototype, the skilled mold maker must deal with the problem of undercutting; any part of the figurine that projects too far from the main portion will break off when the piece is decanted from the mold. To overcome this problem, the manufacturers used multipart molds or would mold certain pieces separately, adding them after the piece had been removed from the mold, but prior to the first firing. Molds had to be constantly replaced, wearing out usually after fifty to one hundred castings. The cast piece was smaller than the prototype, and if a mold was then taken of this piece, the resulting figurine was a size smaller. This allowed German manufacturers to offer the same figurine in several different sizes. Different versions of the same model could also be made by adding bits of clay or scraping away portions of the original, and then making a new mold. Thus the same basic model may be found both nude and with molded swimwear or wigged and with molded hair. This saved the thrifty German manufacturer the expense of creating an entirely new prototype, yet allowed a factory to expand its line to appeal to as wide a market as possible.

Casting was the next step. While early doll heads were produced by rolling the clay material like cookie dough and pressing it into the mold, during the period covered by this book, a liquid slip was being used. Slip is composed of clay that has been ground, sifted, and mixed with other substances and minerals, such as feldspar, which ensures even shrinkage during drying or firing. The slip had to be constantly worked to prevent settling and to sieve out impurities. Such impurities, known as slag, would appear as black specks on the surface of the figurine (and because this slag is part of the figurine, the collector should never try to pick it out, since the result will be at best a chip, and there is a risk of breaking the treasured piece). The slip was poured into molds of plaster of Paris, which absorbed the excess moisture. When the desired thickness of clay had set, the excess liquid was poured off and the figurine removed from the mold.

The damp, thin walled clay piece, which is referred to as "greenware," requires the most careful handling, as it can be easily damaged. Yet, during this stage, the figurine must be handled, for this is when mold lines must be smoothed, openings between the arms or legs cleaned, holes poked through, numbers and trademarks incised if they were not made part of the mold, mold debris removed, and any separately cast pieces, such as arms and legs, added. To add a piece, each part is dabbed with a bit of slip at the place of joining and then firmly pressed together. Not only is there a risk of warping or crushing the delicate greenware, any air pockets carelessly left between the joined pieces can cause the figurine to explode during firing. Yet, no matter how skilled the joining, even in the finest pieces the point of application will be marked by a faint ring or line. Obviously, the more complicated the piece, the more work required, and the better and more expensive the item was. Bathing beauties and nudies can be categorized somewhat like half dolls. The most common are those made in a single two part mold with the arms molded to the body, while the better ones have openings between one or both arms and torso (and, in the case of bathing beauties and nudies, also sometimes between the legs), but with the arms returning to the body and the legs still being joined. The most desirable figurines have one or more limbs that are completely free of the body or other limbs and may have required separate application. The greenware pieces were then allowed to dry completely and "finished," a painstaking dusty process during which the piece is cleaned and smoothed with bits of damp and dry sponge or cloth and features sharpened with special artist tools.

After finishing, the piece is ready for firing. The German manufacturers used high firing kilns, with reported temperatures of up to 2700 degrees Fahrenheit. These enormous kilns, capable sometimes of holding thousands of pieces, took many hours to fill and firings may have taken as long as a week. Successfully firing so many pieces in coal stoked kilns without modern equipment required great skill and knowledge (and some physical risk). Underfiring or overfiring can warp or destroy pieces, and even minor firing problems can cause defects such as kiln lines or a mildew-like speckling in the bisque. Removed from the kiln, the

pieces were rough, requiring vigorous sanding to obtain the satiny smoothness of the best German bisque (modern slip and equipment produce a bisque of almost soapy, poreless smoothness, while even the finest old pieces have a slight drag when a finger is passed along the bisque). Like the finishing on the greenware pieces, this produces a fine dust that factory workers, in poorly ventilated workrooms, would breathe for hours a day. The piece was then bathed to remove any dust and sent on to be decorated.

Originally, the slip was uncolored, so the piece was stark white, requiring a complexion coat that had to be expertly dabbed on and smoothly applied by a skilled worker with a pad of wool wrapped in silk. Some persons have insisted that the even complexions of many of these pieces could only have been achieved with the use of an airbrush. The airbrush, also called a spraygun, was invented by English artist Charles L. Burdick in 1893. The airbrush allows the artist to lay down fine, even, seamless layers of opaque or translucent color not possible with a brush, and Mr. Burdick used his invention for backgrounds in his paintings. However, the Royal Academy of Art rejected his work as being produced mechanically and Mr. Burdick went on to found the Fountain Brush Company. By the turn of the century, photographers were already using the spraygun to retouch photographs and postcards. Airbrushes were used to decorate bisque and china and a number of pieces in my collection from the 1920s have airbrushed decorative touches. Extensive use of the spraygun to decorate figurines does not seem to appear prior to the mid to late 1920s. The spraygun produces a fine mist, and areas so decorated have an even, dense color that is hazy or blurred at the edges. It is possible an airbrush may have been used to apply the complexion on some figurines, but for the most part, the complexion coats seem to have been padded on, which gives the translucent color and varying tones and hues similar to human skin. Once the complexion coat was dry, the figurine could be fired a second time at a lower temperature to fire in the complexion coat, and then featured and refired, or, to save time (and, consequently money), the features painted over the dry complexion coat and fired. Firing permanently sets the colors and, depending on the intensity of colors or complexity of design, several firings might be required.

However, just prior to World War I, and extensively thereafter, German manufacturers began to use a precolored slip, so that fired pieces already had a pinkish tint. This eliminated the costly and time-consuming step of complexion coating. Some manufacturers even went a penny-pinching step further and did not fire the features, so that they washed off or wore away with time. While a tinted bisque piece will be white anywhere it is not complexion-coated, a precolored bisque piece will be the same color all the way through, as can be discovered by looking inside, if possible, or examining any chips or scrapes. Precoloring lacks the depth and warmth of fine tinted bisque, the colors are often muddier as they are painted on a pink, instead of a white, background, and later pieces often have an unpleasant pink greasy color (this harsh sheen should not be confused with the desirable "oily" bisque sometimes found in fine tinted pieces that gives the impression of gleaming, just washed skin). Collectors should avoid scrubbing precolored pieces for, if the features are not fired, a vigorous bath will wash them away.

China is basically bisque which has been glazed, and the same model may have been offered in both bisque and china. The glaze could be applied to the greenware piece and fired, the features then being painted with colors that would penetrate the glaze during the second firing, or the features could be painted first and then fired, the glaze being applied afterwards. Many factories seem to have preferred the first method, as it allowed them to cull out pieces that were warped or damaged in firing before the time-consuming process of decorating. Occasionally a china piece might be found with its features worn away, suggesting the manufacturer saved a few pennies by glazing the piece, then decorating it, but eliminating the second firing.

Once complete, the products were inspected and readied for market. While a modern doll artist might destroy all but the most perfect of his or her creations, the Germans were in a competitive business, and minor flaws that could be hidden by a wig or clothing, or would not otherwise hurt the item's sales appeal, were often passed through inspection. After all, these handmade, mass produced, and often fairly inexpensive, novelty pieces were made in factories without modern equipment, lighting, or ventilation by workers paid meager sums to toil long hours in often dangerous health threatening conditions. Today's collector should not be hypercritical of the occasional kiln line under an arm or a speck of slag in a thigh, but instead amazed that so many of these pieces display such fine workmanship and exquisite beauty. Regarding wigged and dressed bathing beauties and other ladies, some catalogues of the period show that the manufacturers offered fully wigged and dressed products. However, they also sold nude, and even bald, figurines for jobbers to purchase, wig, and dress, and then sell, these middle men adding a few pennies to the price for their profit. Figurines may also have been sold nude to the public, either to dress or tie to pincushions, or to admire as is.

Illustration MM1. Clever use of molding techniques allowed German manufacturers to create many different sizes and versions from one prototype. These figurines appear in the William Goebel section of the "Ladies With a Past" chapter.

From Victoria to Vamp

Naughties, nudies, and bathing beauties are a family of risqué bisque figurines whose popularity stretched from the Gay Nineties through the Roaring Twenties. Although the Victorian home had its share of nude women in bisque or china, their quasi-classical poses and modest demeanor supposedly qualified them as art. However, with the Edwardians came a demand for figurines of scantily or unclad women who made no pretense of being Venus or a Greek slave.

The first two decades of this century were a casting off, both figuratively and literally, of the perceived restraints of the Victorians. Women's fashions changed dramatically during these years, the confining corset and layers of undergarments discarded for slim, clinging dresses whose hemlines began to climb. Women sought more freedom in both fashion and society. Outdoor activities and athletics, for both men and women, were encouraged and a culture of body awareness developed. There was a craving for youth and the rejection of all that was considered repressive and old fashioned, especially after the devastation of World War I. The German porcelain houses sought to profit from this change in attitude. Coyly posed bathing beauties in fashionable and abbreviated swimsuits began to appear in china and bisque. Some of these had painted suits or were dressed in bits of real lace or net, but others were left nude. In addition to these "nudies," there were ladies in their undergarments, the earliest in white chemises and black stockings, their later sisters wearing only sheer stockings and high heels. Some naughty figurines appeared to be an innocent knick-knack until turned over, when they revealed a risqué twist. There were also hollow bisque figurines that, when filled with water, squirted from an appropriate orifice. Although some antique dealers optimistically use the name "Victorian naughties," and many of these items do wear white chemises or nightshirts, black stockings, and split knickers that seem to recall an earlier era, most naughties, nudies, and bathing beauties can be safely dated somewhere between the early years of this century through the 1930s.

While many of the bisque and china bathing beauties, nudies, and naughties are unmarked, there were two major changes in the fashionable woman's silhouette during the early years of this century that can be used to estimate the date of manufacture. Prior to 1900, the favored figure was the matronly hourglass, with its full bosom, nipped in waist, and rounded hips. This unnatural figure was achieved by unnatural means, a corset that forced down the abdomen and crushed the internal organs. Although the faints and frailty of the wealthy Victorian woman were encouraged by society and exaggerated by literature, they had their basis in the constricting corset, which compressed the diaphragm and made taking a deep breath a difficulty; in extreme cases, women suffered broken ribs and crushed spleens in the name of beauty. Yet, the armor-like corset was praised, not only because within its confines each woman could have a "perfect" figure, but also because it served to support a woman's weak flesh and rein in her willing spirit. Tight lacing was a sign of morality, for only a loose woman dared loosen her stays. An upper class woman could not dress or undress herself without aid; she needed a staff of servants to dress her, as well as sew, wash, starch, iron, and repair her elaborate outfits. One wonders if some proper Victorian belle indignantly turned down an illicit rendezvous simply because the prospect of getting dressed and undressed with no assistance but that of an ardent lover was too much trouble to be worth the price of passion. But while society and religion supported the corset, medical science and progressive thinkers condemned it. Doctors attacked the corset as detrimental to the health of women, as did the Rational Dress Society, and the Pre-Raphaelites scorned it as unaesthetic. In 1900, Doctor Franz Glenard and Madame Gaches Sarraute, a corsetiere who had studied medicine, developed the health corset. Said to be modeled on more natural lines, the new corset was designed to support the abdomen, yet free the diaphragm and reduce pressure on the internal organs. However, once again fashion superseded sense, and women continued to tightly lace the waist, producing a figure that is best described as S-shaped, with an exaggerated out-thrust bosom, tiny waist, and counterbalancing hips and derriere. Even the paintings, postcards, and figurines of nude or bathing suited women of the period reflect this odd stance.

This S-shaped silhouette was immortalized by Charles Dana Gibson and his fellow artists, Howard Chandler Christy and Harrison Fisher. Gibson sketched and painted tall, proud, patrician women whose figures were considered to be more modern and youthful than their Victorian predecessors'. Yet, theirs was still a matronly figure, with its emphasis on a full bosom and rounded hips. Cascades of lace (or, for those less favored by nature, padding and bodice boners) defined a full, and oddly single, bosom, for never was there any hint of the separation of the breasts, even in the deep décolleté of the Gibson girl evening gown. A bell shaped skirt cut close to the hips and flaring to the ground and huge feather hats on high piled hair only seemed to emphasize the forward projection of the mono-bosom. French fashion designer Paul Poiret scathingly described the silhouette as dividing "...its wearer into two distinct masses; on the one side there was the bust...on the other, the whole behindward aspect, so that the lady looked as if she was hauling a trailer." The fashionable woman was still secured in stays and whalebone beneath her many layers of petticoats and still needed a trained staff to assist her in

Illustration F1. 4in (10cm) by 6in (15cm) printed silk given as a premium by cigarette companies.

Illustration F2. 4in (10cm) by 6in (15cm) printed silk given as a premium by cigarette companies.

dressing and undressing, often changing her outfit as many as five times a day. However, as elegant as the Gibson girl looked on paper, it is doubtful flesh and blood women achieved the same grace. Heavy hats would go awry, hair would slide free of its hairpins and rats, lace would wilt, and all too human flesh would protrude from the corset edges, as a woman, contorted into a kangaroo posture, moved like an automaton on feet unseen under a heavy skirt. Yet, with new medical emphasis on the importance of exercise and the outdoors, the poor encased Gibson girl was expected to engage in athletics. Gibson and his contemporaries mercilessly sketched her posed with tennis rackets, golf clubs, oars, bicycles, and walking sticks, and many women gamely attempted to comply. Bathing was a popular activity for such artists to portray, languorous beauties posed on windy beaches. Indeed, these early bathing beauties are charming with their high piled hair tied in blowing scarfs, rounded arms revealed by puffed sleeves, tiny waists, and full skirts exposing a length of lithe leg decorously clad in stockings, dainty feet in delicate ballet style bathing slippers. Both coy and provocative, the Gibson girl inspired bather began to appear on postcards, plates, in figurines, and other such decorative paraphernalia. *Illustrations F1 and F2* are two tobacco silks, which suggest they were aimed mainly to-

wards men, as around the turn of this century smoking for the female gender was confined to the fallen woman and floozy. Smaller silks, chromolithographed with subjects from actresses to zoology, were included in cigarette packages, while larger silks, such as these 4in (10cm) by 6in (15cm) examples, could be obtained by mailing in coupons included in the cigarette packs. The seated lady, captioned "Nantucket," wears a suit of soft green trimmed with pink, a matching headdress, and black stockings. The other, entitled "Ormond Beach," is vivid in her brilliant red swimming dress and matching stockings. Such silks were first produced about 1900. Judging by these ladies' bathing garb, they probably were manufactured between 1900 and 1910. Yet as modest as this swimming outfit was, it did expose more limb than ordinary dress, and such bathers became popular subjects of leering jibes. *Illustration F3* is a plate produced in England that copies and lampoons Gibson's style. Marked "F&V.I." in a rectangle over "England//Copyright//Applied For," it shows two dainty beauties posed coyly on the sands in full Gibson girl swim attire, from their full tresses letting fall a few teasing tendrils to stockinged legs displaying slender ankles. "Wont (sic) you please teach us to swim?" they ask the ogling gentleman, and well they might ask. For all the athletic portrayals of the

Gibson girl, swimming was something she probably did not do. As delightful as the early bathing suits were with their jaunty sailor collars and puffed sleeves, they were not meant to be swum in. Of serge or woven wool, they became heavy, sagging, and immodestly clinging when wet. Dyes ran, or even became transparent, and the fabric sometimes shrank at an embarrassingly rapid rate. A wet bathing suit could weigh as much as thirty pounds. A bold woman might skip in the waves up to her knees, but only a foolhardy one would swim. Mr. Edwin Sandy reported of his 1902 attempt to paddle in a woman's bathing suit: "Not until then did I rightly understand what a serious matter a few feet of superfluous cloth might become in water. The suit was amply large, yet pounds of apparently dead weight seemed to be pulling at me in every direction. In that gear a swim of 100 yards was as serious a task as a mile in my own suit. After that experience, I no longer wondered why so few women swim well, but rather that they are able to swim at all."

However, the first decade of this century was to see yet another abrupt change in the ideal female silhouette. Mariano Fortuny, inspired by the sixth century bronze of the Delphi charioteer, created a multi-pleated silk gown. The Delphos dress was not only elegant in its simplicity, but was easy to care for, as it was stored rolled up in a special container. French designer Paul Poiret, influenced, like Fortuny, by an odd mixture of Grecian drapery, Venetian art, Empire gowns, and the Arabian nights (and some say the fact his wife was unfashionably tall and slim), sought to replace the

Illustration F3. 8in (20cm) wide plate. Marked "F&V.I.//England//Copyright//Applied For."

rigid S-shape with softer draping and a more natural elongated line. "I waged war on the corset, I liberated the abdomen," declared the designer, though he did not so much liberate the female as shift the location of her restricting undergarments. The long column like figure so necessary for the graceful draping of rich fabrics required a girdle that began below the breasts, conforming more naturally to the waist, but narrowing the hips and sometimes extending to the midthigh. Some fashionable women were unable to move or sit comfortably with this more "natural" line. Describing a parade of models in a fashion salon of the time in "The Master," Colette declared, "They progress with difficulty, knees joined and bound, and cut through the air as though it was heavy water, helping themselves with their hands, which paddle the air at hip level. These are lovely creatures, whose every deformity has its grace: they no longer have any rumps — the curve is gone from the small of their backs accentuating their length: where does the stomach begin? Where are the breasts hiding?"

Breasts were hiding behind brassieres, made necessary by the lowered girdle that did not support breasts and sheerer fabrics. A descendant of the bodice boner, the brassiere soon was used to de-emphasize what its predecessor exaggerated, combining with a straight girdle to produce a tubular shape. The brassiere first appeared in *Vogue* in 1907 and in 1913 debutante Mary Phelps Jacob was granted a patent for her soft brassiere made without boning, and baring the midriff (Ms. Phelps constructed her prototype brassiere out of handkerchiefs with the assistance of her maid). The move was away from the matronly mono-bosom to, as the protagonist declares in Colette's "My Corset Maker," "the chest of a youth."

Yet another restriction was imposed by Poiret, for after liberating woman from her corset, he then bound her ankles. His hobble skirt of 1910 was so narrow, the wearer could walk only with tiny, mincing steps, like those of a Japanese geisha. Women actually wore a hobble or garter around their ankles to keep them from taking too long a stride and tearing their skirts. One French paper ran a cartoon showing a sketch of a hobbled horse with a fashionable woman, the caption reading "pauvre cheval, pauvre femme." The fad was shortlived, and, on the whole, the decade was one of the gradual freeing of women from the tyranny of restricting clothing.

The 1910s through the 1920s saw the discarding of the layers of underclothing once a staple of women's fashion, even to the linings of dresses, as a slender, more youthful figure became the style. Skirts also were becoming shorter, and the heavy black or white textured stockings of the Gibson girl were replaced by sheerer ones of silk, often colored to compliment the dress. This simplicity in line was not necessarily reflected in the colors of the clothing, as the demure hues and patterns of earlier fashion were replaced by the brilliant, violent colors taken from the canvases of the Fauvists and geometric designs taken from Cubists. Pre-war fashion was exotic and extravagant. Adapting the ethnic, ancient, and Eastern to Western tastes, Poiret dressed women

Illustration F4. Embossed German postcard, marked Series 583. Colored, divided back.

Illustration F5. Embossed German postcard, marked Series 583. Colored, divided back.

Illustration F6. Embossed German postcard, marked Series 583. Colored, divided back.

Illustration F7. Embossed German postcard, marked Series 583. Colored, divided back.

Illustration F8. 12in (31cm) tall cardboard advertising display. Caption reads, "Why don't you get into the swim? The Breakers. Galveston, Tex."

like odalisques, ironic at a time when so many women were seeking greater freedom and the Suffragettes fought for the right of women to vote. Tunics, often sheer to expose the rich fabric of the straight skirt underneath, were the staple of his designs. The Gibson girl pompadour gave way to the chignon worn low on the neck, often wound with Grecian influenced fillets or topped for evening wear by a turban or aigrette of feathers or jewels. In 1911, he threw an extravaganza called the One Thousand and Second Night with hundreds of guests entering an estate transformed into what, to the European imagination, represented the exotic East. Among Oriental carpets, an Eastern bazaar, Nubian slaves, and flamingos, ruled Poiret in the outfit of a pasha, his wife, in lowcut dress and jeweled aigrette, gowned as the sultana. Fashionable women clamored to be clad as harem slaves. The same year saw the introduction of the deep v-neck décolleté, at first filled in modestly with tulle or lace, then later left open. As daring for 1911 was the jupe-culotte, a garment consisting of either harem-like pants worn under a split tunic or a full skirt tapering to trousers; the less bold could wear a dress with a hem split like a fishtail, the ends of which could be wrapped between the legs to create a pantlike affect. In 1913, Poiret introduced the "minaret" skirt, originally created for the ballet "Les Minarets," a panniered outfit which resembled a woman wearing a lampshade about her hips. This perpetual costume party was not always successful, as can be seen from Colette's description of her fashionable, and often ludicrous, friend, Valentine, in "Rites."

A colorist's heated and barbaric imagination lavished this fabric with orange and purple, the green of Venetian necklaces, and the blue-black of sapphires, intermingled with gold....Then a woman came along — my friend Valentine came along — and cried out, "I'm Scheherazade too — like everybody else!"

She struts in front of me, in knock-kneed rhythm. She has loaded down her light, blonde beauty with everything befitting a sultana as pale and round as the moon. A precious and tear-shaped jewel from the Orient sparkles between her eyebrows, astonished that with its glimmering fires it should extinguish two Western eyes of a modest blue. What is more, my friend has just fixed a long aigrette sprinkled with stardust on her head...

The peris, in the Persian paradise, had both this star on their foreheads and this wispy cloud. But my friend's feet disappear under a very Greek petticoat, with regular and supple pleats, tightened at the knees with Hindu drapery. Her hand teases and tucks the squared-off Byzantine sash with beaded Egyptian designs.

Satisfied and serious, she admires herself, without suspecting that something is happening to her...Well, for heaven's sake, it is the same thing that happens to so many young Parisiennes with light complexions, pointed noses and chins, poor skin, and thin eyelashes, as soon as they disguise themselves as Asian princesses: she looks like a little maid.

World War I defeated this frivolity of fashion. As women engaged in volunteer and war work, the tunic was discarded and wider, ankle length skirts gave women more freedom of movement. Shortages resulted in the elimination of lace and trimmings, and by 1918 designers were limited to using no more than four and a half yards of material in a dress. Practical and plain were patriotic. Chemise dresses that hung straight from the shoulder, often with pockets (a

Illustration F9. Black and white postcard, undivided back. Caption reads, "Come and Play with Me."

Come and Play with Me.

practical touch previously thought unnecessary in women's dress), garbed the women working in factories and hospitals.

After the war, there was to be no return to the extravagance of earlier times. Nations were devastated, fortunes lost, and not only would wrapping oneself in jewels and rich fabrics be considered gauche, it could brand one as a war profiteer. The war had introduced women to a world outside of that of home and fashion. Culture, politics, and even careers, held greater interest than the couturier's shop. In 1919, Great Britain would enfranchise married women over thirty, and the following year the United States would grant the vote to its female citizens. Further, the loss of so many young men in the trenches and battlefields meant many young women would not marry, once the inevitable, and only, state to which a proper young lady could aspire. The horror of so much death begat a cult for youth and athletics. Women took their place again on the beaches, golf links, and tennis courts, but to compete, not pose. Dresses became shorter and looser, and women copied the masculine garb as well, with pyjamas and tailored suits. The lithe, adolescent form was the silhouette, to the point of androgyny. Hair was bobbed or covered with tight fitting cloches, breasts and hips hidden, as the long, lean leg became the new erogenous zone. For the young and slim, all undergarments were discarded except for a garterbelt, while the less fashionably formed squeezed into girdles and flattened their breasts. Oddly, while the form was boyish, the face was not, as obvious cosmetics became acceptable for women at all levels of society, such powders and potions previously being restricted to the scandalous painted lady. By the mid 1920s, although the silhouette was still slim, it was more natural. Hints of curves began to reappear and the brassiere, previously a flattener, was now used to support and shape the bustline. Hair became longer, and hemlines lowered, as

the world moved from the horrors of war and the almost frantic gaiety of the flappers to the sobering crash of 1929.

These rapid shifts in fashion were also reflected in women's swimwear. Picturesque bathing was giving way to swimming. A tunic suit worn over bathing shorts, the successor of the Gibson girl suit with its skirts and bloomers, would survive, although becoming ever briefer, through the 1920s. *The Delineator* in August of 1915 offered two patterns for bathing suits, one with an empire waist and the other a "princess" style with attached knickerbockers, both with matching bathing hats. The suggested materials were satin, taffeta, mohair, brilliantine, or peau de soie. In 1900, American swimmer Annette Kellerman wore a one piece tank suit and by 1910 it was accepted attire on most American beaches. The tank suit became the basic beach fashion, the legs becoming higher and the back lower as the century moved into the sunworshipping of the 1920s.

The figure-skimming tank suit seems to have brought new life to the bathing beauty craze. There was a plethora of postcards, prints, advertising, and figurines of ladies in this revealing (for the time) outfit. *Illustrations F4 through F7* are from a series of beautifully embossed German postcards showing women in elaborate swimsuits, adorned in some cases with laces and ribbons, and others with surprising décolleté and peek-a-boo lacings on the legs. These suits seem to represent a transition from the Gibson girl frou-frou to the sleek tank suits of the twenties, as some still retain hints of nautical collars and skirts, while others are daringly simple. Although these postcards are unused, I have seen cards from the same series postmarked 1908. *Illustration F8* shows the same theme adopted for advertising. 12in (31cm) tall and beautifully colored, it folds out to display two bathers descending from a wheeled bathing house (originally developed during Victorian times, these wheeled carts not only provided a place for a lady to change, but were pulled out into the waves so she could enter the sea unseen). The caption reads, "Why don't you get into the swim? The Breakers. Galveston, Tex." The Breakers was one of several large bath houses in Galveston, which gave patrons a place to change and swim. It was first listed in the Galveston directory in 1906, and the style of the swimsuits suggest this delightful advertising giveaway dates somewhere between then and 1910. The question these lovely paper items raise is whether such wonderful fashion confections really existed, or are just wistful thinking by a male artist trapped in some dank studio.

Illustration F9 is an early photo postcard of a young model in a body defining tank suit. The pose, and the ballet tied bathing slippers (worn with stockings), are similar to those found in her three dimensional bisque sisters. "Come play with me", reads the caption, as she gives a sly smile to the camera. Her suit appears to be strapless, and although the author has seen at least one other bathing beauty postcard adorned with a strapless suit, it is unlikely such an outfit ever saw the seashore; unless it was either wired or glued on, it would have been impossible to keep decently in place. The back of the card is undivided, in that there is not separation between the address and message portions. As this appears to be an American card (in the corner for postage, it instructs that domestic is one cent, foreign two cents), this would date it prior to 1907, which was the year the United States, following the example of Europe, introduced the divided back postcard.

Illustration F10 is another undivided back American photo postcard. Captioned "The Venus Raft", it displays a bevy of real bathing beauties wearing swim attire resembling that displayed in *Illustrations F4 through F7* (note the woman sitting on the far left corner wears a suit identical to *Illustration F8's*, only this suit has straps. For the first postcard, the photographer may have retouched out the

straps, or simply tucked them into the suit, for a more alluring picture). Unless the photographer was handy with a needle or went to the expense of having this wardrobe specially made, one must assume these are real swim suits, with their daring decolletage, bared backs, form fitting fit, and the lacing that leaves little leg to the imagination. Though these suits are more swimable than the earlier attire, this charming scene obviously took place at a photography studio and not the beach. None of the suits show the slightest evidence of damp, nor would the elaborate hair bows or the delightful hat have survived a swim. All the women appear to be wearing stockings, but only one has donned a black pair (the diver in the lace trimmed swimwear has rolled hers down to her ankles, a foreshadowing of the turned down hose of her flapper daughters?). Again, many of these poses would appear in the bathing beauty figurines as well.

Such suits would have no doubt been greeted with shock on many American beaches in the early years of our century, at least by the female population. However, *Illustration F11* suggests men were not quite so scandalized by the ever briefer swimming attire. Postmarked August 1, 1908, it was sent from Amarillo, Texas, by a gentleman to a male acquaintance in Peabody, Kansas (I have a number of bathing beauty postcards, and many seem to have been sent by men to men, neither sender or sendee living in a town known for its beaches or lakeside resorts). Three smiling ladies in brightly striped tank suits and beflowered hats pose by a painted lake. On the back, the sender has written, "On the other side kindly note the latest abbreviation for Bathing Suit & be governed accordingly." *Illustration F12*, a printer's sample for a 1921 "art calendar," shows how simple and sleek swimsuits had become by the early 1920s. Here, the young lady's hat is far fancier than her form fitting suit. The special 1931 commemorative envelope from Saint Petersburg, Florida shown in *Illustration F13* demonstrates that

Illustration F11. Postcard postmarked August 1, 1908. Tinted photograph, divided back.

little change took place in the basic tank suit during the ensuing decade, other than the shortening of the leg, enlarging of the armholes, and lowering of the back.

The changes in fashion, morals, and a woman's place in society are amusingly summarized in *Illustration F14*. This colored comic strip, from the June 6, 1926, edition of the *Tampa Daily News*, was drawn by Chic Young, best known as the creator of Blondie and Dagwood. In two succinct panels, Mr. Young symbolizes all the change and chaos of the past two decades. "When Mother Was A Girl" shows demure Gibson girls in high collared shirtwaists discretely waltzing with their respectful beaus under the forbidding gaze of a chaperone. "But Daughter — Oh!" displays flappers in short hair and shorter skirts bunnyhugging with their sheiks on a moonlight beach, nary a duenna in sight. Talk about generation gaps! The accompanying strip, "Joe College," lampoons how far (or high) swimsuits had come by the mid 1920s.

Illustration F12. Printer's sample for 1921 "art calendar."

Illustration F13. 1931 commemorative envelope from Saint Petersburg, Florida.

Illustration F14. Comic strip by Chic Young from June 6, 1926, edition of *Tampa Daily News*.

Crowning Glory

Probably the prize of any bathing beauty collection is the mohair wigged bather or nudie. Some people credit these little figurines as French, a carry over from the early days of doll collecting when only the French were considered capable of producing the most exquisite and finest bisque dolls. However, research has shown that not only did the French produce some very inferior products, the German manufacturers possessed the skill and artistry to produce dolls so fine they were shipped to France to be sold in the most exclusive French toy stores. The translucent bisque head of the "French" bebe in her silk and ribbons may well have come from a German firm such as Simon and Halbig. Almost every German firm advertised bathing beauties among their products and catalogues from such firms as Kestner and Galluba and Hofmann contain pictures of dainty damsels in mohair wigs. Produced in some form by nearly every German bisque manufacturer of the period, these delicate, delightful ladies all have dainty mohair wigs over solid dome heads, slim bodies in eloquent poses, finely painted features, and usually either molded one strap or ballet type bathing slippers. Although these figurines may have been sold nude, many were originally dressed in swimsuits of silk net or lace, but the years may have unraveled the rather revealing swimsuits. Often all that is left for the lucky collector is the wig with the frail remains of the bathing cap and a shredded suit with frayed ribbons.

Illustration CG1 is one of the most sought after of these figurines, two beautiful bathers molded together in one pose. 4½in (12cm) tall, these tantalizing twins both have their original glossy brown mohair wigs in the typical style found on many bathers with a stitched center seam and the long hair pulled back and tucked in to form a loose roll. They also both have dark brown brows, sultry intaglio blue eyes with red lid lines and upper and lower black lid lines, black pupils with white highlight dots, deep coral nose dots, and parted coral smiling lips with a slightly darker center line. Modeling such a complex pose took great skill and a number of molds. The application lines are difficult to trace in the finely finished bisque, partially because of a reluctance to disturb the fragile remains of the original swimsuits. However, not only were the two ladies separately molded, on the upper figurine it appears the left arm, ending in a dainty hand with free thumb, and right leg were added. The right arm also seems to have been added, and was actually molded as part of the shoulder of the lower lady. As for the bottom belle, her right arm and leg were apparently molded separately and added in the greenware stage; her left arm was also added, and, as the hand seems to have been molded with the right shin, may have been part of the right leg mold. Both

bathers have molded one strap bathing slippers, pink for the top figure, blue for the lower. Of fine pale peachy bisque, for all their excellent modeling and workmanship, these ladies display an anatomical flaw common to many of the mohair wigged women; in elongating the torso and limbs to create the complex and graceful poses, the head becomes far too small for the body. This fault is hidden by the full wigs, but when seen bald, these bathers are rather microcephalic. This exquisite example is incised only "851." underneath. The upper lady retains the remains of her silk net swimsuit, now faded taupe, but once a bright silver blue with golden yellow ribbons, while her patient companion's dingy yellow shredded suit was originally bright golden yellow with lavender bows.

Another playful scene, probably by the same maker, consists of a laughing woman lying on her back while her female friend, who stands between her upraised legs, pulls her along by her ankles. There is also a double figurine consisting of a seated swimmer on a molded bench whose companion stands beside her. These doubles come in several sizes, and while the quality does vary, they are all extremely unusual and collectible.

Bathing beauties doing anything other than simply simpering are very desirable, and *Illustration CG2's* size and near mint condition make her even more so. 8in (20cm) long, she retains her dark brown mohair wig and net swim cap and suit, now dull orange, but once bright pinkish red decorated by green-gold ribbons. The excellent facial decoration is typical of so many of these beautiful bathers: dark brown one stroke brows; blue intaglio eyes with red lid lines, upper and lower black lid lines, large black pupils and white highlights; deep coral nose dots; and, coral lips, in this case parted to display slightly molded teeth. *Illustration CG3* is a closeup of her lovely face. The right arm was added at the shoulder and the left arm was added at the elbow. Her right leg was added at the hip. The molded book has a red-brown cover, blue edged pages, and faint black "writing," and her light blue ballet type bathing slippers are tied in bows at the ankles. The bisque is pale peach and beautifully finished, but if she is marked, it is hidden under her suit. In this case the book was molded as part of the pose, but in another series of bathers who are accompanied by a small spotted cat or dog, the pet was molded separately and simply added to a stock bather, so that often the figurine appears completely unaware of the kitten or puppy that seems to be clawing its way up her bare leg. Whether the object was conceived as part of the position, or was added as a creative afterthought, any such wigged lady is collectible.

Illustration CG1. 4½in (12cm) tall bisque figurine of two women. Original mohair wigs and remains of original net swimsuits. Incised "851" underneath.

(Above)
Illustration CG2. 8in (20cm) long bisque figurine. Original mohair wig and net swimsuit. No visible marks.

Illustration CG3. Closeup of the face of *CG2*.

5¼in (13cm) long, *Illustration CG4* still retains her original blonde mohair wig, a change from the usual brunette, and her net swimwear, now dull deep pink with greenish yellow ribbons, but once shimmering bright pink trimmed in golden bows. Of pale slightly oily bisque, which gives her a just scrubbed sheen (and not to be confused with the unpleasant shine of late precolored bisque), this popular pose is found in a number of sizes. Her one stroke brows are dull black and her sultry blue eyes are painted with the same detail as *Illustration CG2's*. She also has coral nose dots and her very full lips are slightly parted. *Illustration CG5* is a closer view of her head and shoulders, revealing amazing artistry. Both her graceful arms were added at the shoulders and her lithe legs at the hips. Her molded ballet type slippers are pale blue, but they have also been seen in pink and white. Although any maker should have been proud to claim her, she is incised on her bottom only with what appears to read "No. 508" and a small elongated rectangle.

Illustration CG6, of pale, almost white bisque (all these wigged bathers are so fair it is hard to believe they really represent beach belles), shows how time takes its toll on the delicate bathing suits of silk net. Originally bright yellow trimmed in purple ribbons, the remaining raiment is now dingy yellow, the bows faded almost to brown. Her mohair wig is dark brown and her facial features match those of the preceding ladies', except her bowed lips are closed. *Illustration CG7* focuses further on her face. Both her arms were added at the shoulders, and her delicate hands with free thumbs even have creases in the palms and at the finger joints, although such details are hidden by her pose. Both her legs may also have been applied, but examination would risk destroying the frail remains of her original outfit. She wears molded pink one strap slippers. Incised "403 S" on her right buttock, she may be from the fine factory of Galluba and Hofmann which used "400" numbers, often followed by a letter, on its lovely ladies; the chapter entitled "Ladies With a Past" discusses Galluba in more detail. She is both 3in (8cm) tall and long.

Incised "406T" on her right buttock, *Illustration CG8* may also be from Galluba. She wears molded one strap pink slippers and it is tempting to hypothesize that this footwear is a favorite of Galluba, and that *Illustration CG1*, with the same slippers, is also from this factory. However, the section covering Galluba in "Ladies With a Past" also shows that it may have produced bathers with ballet type bathing slippers as well. Her mohair wig is reddish brown and her painted blue eyes are typical, as are her coral nose dots and full parted lips. She also wears her original swimwear, and demonstrates what colorful confections adorned these damsels. Although her cap and ribbons are a faded taupe, originally they were a bright silvery blue and a gleaming pink, respectively, a brilliant contrast to her black lace suit. 4¼in (8cm) long, her left arm was added just below the shoulder, and both legs also appear applied. Her finely modeled hands have dimples at the knuckles, as well as creases in the palms and at the finger joints. *Illustration CG9* better shows her beautiful face.

Another popular pose appears in *Illustration CG10*, who also still wears what remains of her bathing suit of deep pink ribbed silk. 2½in (6cm) tall, she has molded blue one strap slippers and is incised with a "400" number underneath, although the last digit is not legible. Her one stroke light brown brows match her mohair wig, and her facial painting is typical for this type. Of excellent pale bisque, she shares the fine modeling of her bigger sisters, including the hidden details of her hands. It appears both the arms and legs were applied.

Incised underneath with "407" and an elongated rectangle similar to that incised under *Illustration CG4*, *Illustration CG11* may also be from Galluba. 2½in (6cm) tall, her tiny features are decorated with many of the same details of the larger ladies, although her left hand, while it has a free thumb, does not have the molded details on the palm. With her right hand she puts on a white one strap slipper, the heel of which was molded in her hand. Both legs appear to have been applied at the hips, and her arms at the shoulders. Her pale bisque has a slightly oily sheen. The white mohair wig is a replacement and is easy to make. Simply take a hank of mohair and tie a knot. Trim one end, tucking it up into the knot (a dot of white glue will hold it into place), then push this end, like a turban, over the head and form it to the lady's naked dome. The other end can be twisted and tucked through the top of the wig, making a bun.

Although her bathing assemble is not original, *Illustration CG12* shows how even the most unsophisticated seamstress can authentically outfit one of these bathers. Most antique shows have a booth or two that offers a basket or box of lace scraps to rummage through and I lucked upon this lace that not only had enough stretch to shape to a bather's body, but was already trimmed in a fine yellow ribbon similar to that originally used to trim the lace or net swimsuits. The lace fit this beauty perfectly from breast to thigh. I folded the lace over her, tightening it by working the needle back and forth to form a seam underneath. A couple of stitches between her thighs shape the suit's legs. For the straps I carefully worked loose another bit of ribbon, and using a couple of stitches to anchor it at the back, I pulled it forward, tying a bow between her breasts and sewing it in place. In many bathers these bows were not really tied, instead the ribbon was merely looped and stitched into shape. The cap, which was not stitched to her original dark brown mohair wig in order to avoid damage, was made of the same net material; the finished edge was fitted around the head with the excess material folded over where the edges met and stitched in place. Dressing is not an absolute necessity with bathers, as it is with dolls; the first look charming nude while the second look forlorn. However, a bathing cap of antique net or lace can help disguise an original, but thinning, wig or cover the imperfections of a replacement. Because the heads of these bathers are so often out of proportion, baldness distracts from their beauty and a replacement wig of mohair or silk floss may be preferable to a bare pate (human hair and modern synthetic fibers are too coarse and not authentic). 5in (13cm) long, this figure's one stroke brown brows are a shade lighter than her wig and she has the usual fine facial decoration of her type, although she is lacking nose dots. Her arms, with their finely detailed hands, were added at the shoulder and her upraised right leg may also have been applied. Her ballet type slippers are light blue.

Of far more naturalistic proportions than the preceding bathers, *Illustration CG13* shows exaggeration was not necessary to be exquisite. She is beautifully balanced and realistically modeled from every angle, as confirmed by the back view shown in *Illustration CG14*. Her original auburn wig still retains a ribbon of reddish net and her one stroke brows match her hair. She does not have lower lid lines, but as seen in *Illustration CG15*, this does not blemish the beauty of her face. Her bowed lips have a long center line and the square face has a slight double chin. The slender hands have free thumbs and she appears to have just blown a kiss to some admirer. Her lower arms seem to have been applied at the elbows and her left leg at the hip. Of pale flawless bisque, she has molded and slightly blushed nipples, a detail not generally found on bathers whose bountiful breasts were often left as blank as those on the modern fashion dolls. Her light turquoise slippers, which perfectly match her eyes, are also different in that they have a single strap across the front, molded ribbons that wrap and tie at the ankle, and low heels. She is 4½in (11cm) tall and is un-marked.

The 7in (18cm) long figurine in *Illustration CG16* has more natural proportions, excellent bisque, molded and tinted nipples, and the two strap heeled bathing slippers (although her slippers only strap, not wrap and tie, at the ankle) of *Illustration CG13*, which suggests they may be of the same factory. Her light brown mohair wig of long ringlets is old and well made and may be original. The one stroke brows are brown and her half closed painted blue eyes do have lower lid lines, unlike *Illustration CG13*. However, like the preceding illustration, she has the same full lips with elongated center line, squarish face, and slight double chin. *Illustration CG17* better shows her very vamp-ish bedroom eyes. Both her arms were added at the shoulder and her right leg at the hip. She is also unmarked.

5in (13cm) long and 4in (10cm) high, *Illustration CG18* is also different, as she is sans slippers. While factories readily sold ladies "barefoot to the chin", they usually clothed them from ankle down with molded footwear. Her almost white mohair wig is a replacement and was very simple to make. A hank of mohair was folded in half, the fold shaped to the lady's bare dome to form a cap. The rest was braided and wound into an elaborate bun at the back, glued in place and held with pins until dry, and then pulled around the head to finish the hairline. The end here was left to hang down as a ringlet, but it could also have been trimmed and tucked up underneath. Her one stroke brows are dark brown and the painted blue eyes have shallow intaglio black pupils with white highlights, red and black

upper lid lines, and dark brown lower lid lines. The parted lips are deep red. Of rosier bisque than the previous ladies, her very long, lithe legs were added at the hips, her left arm at the shoulder, and the right arm at the elbow. Her hands, although slim and pretty, do not have free thumbs and lack the detail of the preceding beauties', nor does she have the nice anatomical touches, such as dimples in her back. However, she is large, beautifully finished, and different. She is incised "741.0." underneath.

4½in (12cm) tall, *Illustration CG19'*s elegant pose brings to mind a curtsying ballerina. Her blonde wig of silk floss is a replacement. A center seam was sewn with thread as close in color to the hair as possible, the long black hair tied off to form a ponytail that was twisted around itself and tucked up underneath in a manner similar to some of the old wigs. Her one stroke brows are dark brown and her half closed painted blue eyes have red lid lines and are outlined in black. The parted lips are orange red and slightly smiling, but her most striking facial feature is her rather large and prominent nose. The long graceful hands have free thumbs, and both arms were added at the shoulder. The left leg was added at the hip and her right at the knee. She is of beautifully finished peachy bisque and her nipples are molded, but not tinted. The strapless gray slippers are trimmed in black and have deep red brown soles. She is unmarked.

Illustration CG20 is so similar to *Illustration CG18* in appearance (such as the prominent proboscis) and pose, they certainly were part of the same series. 4¾in (12cm) tall, she has been redressed in black antique lace and silk ribbon as a ballerina. She has light brown one stroke brows and her blue painted eyes, which are completely outlined in black, have white highlights as well as red lid lines. Only half of her deep red lips were painted, as the rest are hidden by her right hand. Her arms were added at the shoulders, her right leg at the hip, and her left leg at the knee. The deep pink strapless slippers are trimmed in yellow and have red brown soles. There are no marks.

There is no doubt that *Illustrations CG21 and CG22* are from the same series. 4in (10cm) tall, *Illustration CG21* has her original reddish brown wig pulled back into a chignon. Of natural, less idealized proportions, she has one stroke brown brows, and, under red and black lid lines, she has only black dot eyes with white highlights. Her pursed mouth is brick red. The hands have deeply molded nails with free thumbs and her unusual orange-red bathing slippers have lightly molded ribbons that cross and tie at the ankle. Of excellent pale bisque, her arms and legs were applied. She is incised "3627" on her left buttock.

Incised "3630" under her right thigh, *Illustration CG22* is certainly from the same series and factory. 4in (10cm) tall, her original deep blonde mohair wig is in the same style. Her facial decoration is also the same, although her fuller lips and more oval face give her a softer look. Her hands also have deeply molded nails, and she wears the same bathing slippers in black. *Illustration CG23* gives a back view of her nicely preserved wig and the natural proportions of her softly modeled figure.

Illustration CG4. 5¼in (13cm) long bisque figurine. Original mohair wig and net swimsuit. Incised on her bottom with "No. 508" and an elongated rectangle.

Illustration CG5. Closeup of the face of *Illustration CG4*.

Illustration CG6. 3in (8cm) tall bisque figurine. Original mohair wig and net swimsuit. Incised "403 S" on the right buttock.

Illustration CG7. Closeup of the face of *Illustration CG6*.

Illustration CG8. 4¼in (8cm) long bisque figurine. Original mohair wig, net swim cap, and lace swimsuit. Incised "406T" on her right buttock.

Illustration CG9. Closeup of face of *Illustration CG8.*

Illustration CG10. 2½in (6cm) tall bisque figurine. Original mohair wig and ribbed silk swimsuit. Incised underneath with a "400" number, but the last digit is not legible.

Illustration CG11. 2½in (6cm) tall bisque figurine. Replaced mohair wig. Incised underneath with "407" and an elongated rectangle.

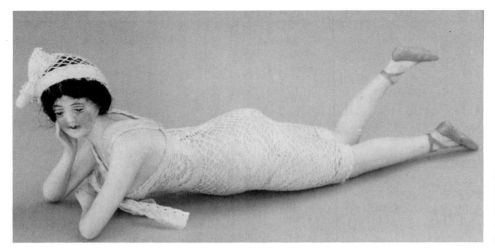

Illustration CG12. 5in (13cm) long bisque figurine. Original mohair wig and replaced lace swimsuit. Unmarked.

(Above Left)
Illustration CG13. 4¼in (11cm) tall bisque figurine. Original mohair wig. Unmarked.

(Above Right)
Illustration CG14. Back view of *Illustration CG13.*

Illustration CG15. Closeup of the face of *Illustration CG13.*

Illustration CG16. 7in (18cm) long bisque figurine. Wig may be original. Unmarked.

Illustration CG17. Closeup of the face of *Illustration CG16*.

Illustration CG18. 5in (13cm) long and 4in (10cm) tall bisque figurine. Replaced wig. Incised "741.0." underneath.

Illustration CG20. 4¾in (12cm) tall bisque figurine. Redressed and rewigged. Unmarked.

26

Illustration CG21. 4in (10cm) tall bisque figurine. Original wig. Incised "3627" on her left buttock.

(Below Left)
Illustration CG22. 4in (10cm) tall bisque figurine. Original mohair wig. Incised "3630" under her right thigh.

(Below Right)
Illustration CG23. Back view of *Illustration CG22*.

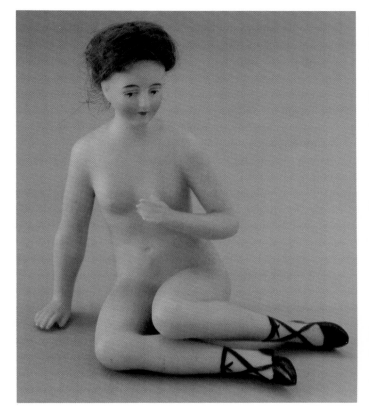

By the Sea

One difficulty facing the collector is when is the lady of his or her attentions a bathing beauty and when is she a nudie? The wigged beauties were sold both nude or suited, and even when originally dressed, many of the silk net or lace swimsuits have succumbed to the ravages of time. Manufacturers of molded hair lovelies have also occasionally tried to increase their products' appeal to the public with costumes of real fabric or lace. Unless one is lucky enough to find a bathing beauty in at least the ragged remains of her original swimsuit, or the figurine is molded in such a way that it would have been impossible to dress her, it is often hard to distinguish the intended bathing beauty from the nudie. There is one situation in which there is absolutely no question, and that is when the maker painted the bathing suit on the bather. William Goebel, as set forth in the chapter entitled "Ladies With A Past," often adorned his ladies in suave striped suits, and throughout this book there are many other examples of swimmers in painted suits. The variety of poses, swimwear styles, and color combinations makes collecting painted suit bathers a delight in and of itself.

Illustration BS1 is quite a contrast to the demure diver in *Illustration BS2*. Sitting before her wicker beach chair, this flapper flaunts her new freedoms, with her bobbed caramel hair, form fitting tank suit, cocky pose, and cigarette held in a defiant gesture (some of her complexion coat was smeared onto her cigarette, so that it appears to be her middle digit and she is making a defiant gesture of quite another sort, but on close examination, I can assure the reader it was meant to be a cigarette). This last detail helps date her; prior to the twenties only the loosest of ladies lit up, thereafter, tobacco, like short hair and skirts or powdered faces and painted lips, became the emblem of the young modern woman. Only 2¾in (7cm) high, this bisque figurine encapsulates the attitude of a new generation. Molded separately from the tan beach chair, she is well detailed and decorated for her size. Her glossy blue bathing cap matches the trim on her white swimsuit (which has molded, but undecorated, horizontal stripes) and slippers, and her complexion coat is pale and even. The one stroke brows are dark blonde, she has black lid lines and pupils, and her heart shaped red mouth seems to form a confident smirk. Unfortunately, her maker lacked her confidence, and she is unmarked.

Illustration BS2 is an early and beautiful example. 6½in (17cm) tall and of excellent sharp bisque, she prepares to dive into the molded waves at her feet (perhaps because this pose so well displays a shapely figure, bathing beauties of all types and eras appear in variations of this position). Her dark blonde hair is pulled into a bun and there is a molded, but undecorated, band across the back of her head. Her one stroke brows match her hair and her blue painted eyes have black lid lines and pupils. The rosy cheeks are dimpled and her finely painted coral mouth hints at a smile. Her suit is light green, shading darker at the neckline and hem, shirred at the yoke and the stomach, a belt with a molded bow defining her trim waist. The back is shirred in a "V" from her waist to her hips, and above there is molded ribbing running from her waist to her shoulders. The front of her suit is trimmed in gold, but her thrifty maker did not waste gilt on the back. Her strapless slippers match the green of her suit. She stands on a gilt edged diving platform that pokes out of dark green and gilded foliage. Swirls of blue water rise under the board, and behind she is supported by a pillar of sandy brick. The peachy complexion is flawless. Her slim arms, which appear to have been added at the shoulder, end in beautifully detailed hands with free thumbs, and a multi-part mold was needed to form her slender legs and complex base. Her manufacturer was thrifty not only with the gold paint, but also its marks, for she bears neither trademark or number.

Illustration BS3's costume is awash in color, perhaps to make up for the fact her complexion was left stark white, without even blush for her cheeks. Her windblown scarf is light blue, the bathing suit pale pink trimmed with bright green bows, and the ballet type slippers are light purple. Of good sharp bisque with excellent modeling, her beautiful face is somewhat marred by a decorator's odd choice of color. Her eyes, with dark brown lid lines, are the same color as her pale blonde hair, as are her parted lips with a dark brown center line. The quality of the decoration is excellent, but she would certainly have been more conventionally pretty with blue eyes and rosy lips. Was this choice of colors intentional, or was there a mistake along the production line? There can be no quarrel, however, with the modeling or finishing. Both arms appear to have been added and the plump little hands with free thumbs could not be prettier. Clever use of mold lines allowed her slim, shapely legs to be molded with her torso. Her pure white complexion is well complemented by her pastel outfit. I have seen a number of high quality bathing beauties left pure white, despite their molded bathing suits, harking back to parian figurines and marble statuary. Perhaps this bather was a manufacturer's experimental transition between these and fully tinted figurines. This could help explain the curious coloring of her face. She is 2¼in (5cm) high.

Precolored bisque was a later development that saved the time and expense of a complexion coat, although many manufacturers still lavished fine modeling and decoration, as well as imagination, on their precolored items. *Illustra-*

tion BS4 is of an excellent precolored bisque that has none of the unattractive greasy pinkish color of many late precolored pieces. 2½in (6cm) tall, she has a large airhole underneath and one can see she is the same flesh tone inside as well as out; otherwise, she could almost pass as tinted bisque. Her Napoleonic beach hat is light green with a bright blue crown, the reddish hair peeking out at the sides. She has brown one stroke brows, large black eyes with black lid lines, rose tinted cheeks, and a delicately painted red mouth with a darker center line. The very pale yellow tank suit is trimmed in black and her slippers are the same faint yellow. The parasol is new but fits into her right hand, which was drilled to hold some object. By keeping her legs and left arm in line with her body, only the right arm needed to be molded separately to avoid undercutting. The modeling, finishing, and decoration are of high quality. She is incised "Germany" on the back of her legs and "GES. GESCH/Sp.1608" across her lower back. Ges. Gesch is not the maker, but is short for "Gesetzlich geschuzt," which means the patent rights had been granted and registered for the design. The "Sp" is puzzling. It is tempting to suggest these are the initials of Sonneberger Porzellanfabrik, but its products are marked by a capital "S" and "P", while here the lower case "p" followed by a period implies this is in fact an abbreviation of a word. Perhaps it is short for some German word, such as "spielfiguren" (play figures), or is simply the manufacturer's catalogue designation for its bathing beauty series. There is another clue. In 1987, an original cardboard display box containing samples of bathing beauties from the factory of Hertel, Schwab and Company, including the same version of this bather, was sold at auction. Beside each bather was a faded paper label with handwritten numbers, which appeared to be the model number and cost, and several of the possible model numbers began with an "Sp." (the paper label by the same model carried the number "2064" and a near mirror version was labeled "2065." I was unable to physically examine the box, so I did not have the opportunity to check what, if any, numbers were incised on the figurines themselves). Founded in 1910, Hertel is best known for its excellent character doll heads, but as late as 1930, it was advertising "tea-cosy shoulderheads, pin-cushions," and no doubt was also producing the associated bathing beauties.

Illustration BS5 was made to sit on a shelf edge, and though she can balance by herself, the slightest jar will shake her from her perch, so I suspect that not too many of this type survived. 3½in (9cm) tall, she is of good quality bisque and modeling. Her slightly glossy bathing cap and ballet type slippers are pale lavender, and the one piece suit, with a molded bow at the bosom and lacing at the thigh, is bright green. Her short curly hair is deep blonde, the one stroke brows dark brown, the eyes and lid lines black, and the pursed lips deep red. In her left hand she holds a square white object, perhaps a purse, that serves as one of her points of balance. Her even complexion is slightly darker than *Illustration BS2's*, as if she has a faint tan. Although she is incised only "12823" on her right hip, in my collection I

have a slightly larger version in china on a powder dish that bears the crown and crosshatched "S" of the Sitzendorf Porcelain Manufactory. The factory, which produced doll heads, porcelain figurines, and decorative pieces, used this mark after the turn of the century. Although the china variation has light blue cap and slippers, a rust colored swimsuit, and blue painted eyes with red and black lid lines, there is no mistaking the unique pose. She sits on a powder dish shaped like a tufted hassock, decorated by a spray gun in orange and blue.

Illustration BS6 may also be a Hertel product. 4in (10cm) tall, she is not only of the same quality precolored bisque as *BS4*, her model number is also preceded by an "Sp." Her dark blue bathing cap has uncolored puffs on each side, as if she has chosen to wear earmuffs to the beach, and only her brown bangs are visible. The features are neatly painted, with brown one stroke brows, blue painted eyes with black lid lines and pupils, and bright red lips. Like *BS4*, she wears a yellow tank suit with black trim, but her slippers are shiny black. The light blue towel draped over her right arm falls to the floor, twisting behind her to form an imaginative pedestal. Her base is trimmed in light red and is incised on the back "GERMANY//Sp.432."

Incised "GERMANY//Sp.433," *Illustration BS7* is clearly part of the same series as the preceding illustration. Of the same fine quality bisque and decoration (as well as size), she wears a deep orange bathing cap topped by a pom-pom, her blonde bangs and a curl on her left cheek peeking out from underneath. The one stroke brows are brown and her black

Illustration BS1. 2¾in (7cm) tall bisque figurine of bathing beauty by a beach chair. Unmarked.

Illustration BS2. 6½in (17cm) tall bisque bathing beauty. Unmarked.

dot eyes have only black lid lines. Her lips are light orange. The suit is pale blue, trimmed in the same orange as her cap, while her slippers match the suit. She stands against a tan wooden pier, wrapped in rope, and the base is trimmed in the same color as *Illustration BS6's.*

Illustration BS8, while also a standing bathing beauty, is a far more common and poorer quality figurine. 3¾in (10cm) tall, she is of very pink precolored bisque with the greasy sheen that seems to plague late precolored bisque pieces. Although she has a molded bathing cap, it was painted the same shiny black as her hair. Her features, which are a little better painted than on many of this type of figurine, are black one stroke brows, black eyes and lid lines, and very red lips. Her suit is light blue trimmed in a darker shade. No attempt was made to cleverly disguise her supporting pedestal as a towel or pier. She was made in a single mold and can be found in a number of variations, such as one hand on her head while the other is at a hip, or her legs crossed at the ankle. She is also found with snow (bits of ground bisque applied with wet slip, giving a pebbly texture) decoration on her suit and bathing cap. In this piece, the colors were fired, but on many similar pieces the manufacturer did not bother with the cost of the second firing, so the colors have rubbed or washed away over the years. Incised only "Germany," she, and many thousands like her, were produced by that country and shipped over to the United States, for she is one of the most often found bathing beauties.

Illustration BS9 may be the most common type of bathing beauty and is frequently found at antique shows and flea markets. 3¼in (8cm) long, she is of very pink greasy precolored bisque. Her green cap and lavender swimsuit have been treated with bisque snow, but she is also found without this treatment, the suit painted a solid color or striped. Her decoration, as on so many of these late, inexpensive items, is hasty, with black dabs of hair sticking out from under her cap, one stroke brows, black lid lines and pupils, orangy mouth, and pink-orange cheeks. The straps of her suit and slippers are red-brown. She is also found in a number of variations, sometimes in a mirror image, the hand at her hip instead of her hair, the cap topped by a pompom, or legs crossed at the ankles. Although the colors in this case are fired in, often they were not, and the features are consequently often faint or completely worn away. She is incised "5684." A 5000 series number appears on many late bathing beauties, suggesting a single prolific manufacturer. *Illustrations BS8 and BS9,* while crudely charming, are not to be confused with finer or earlier bathing beauties. Unfortunately, some antique dealers, upon hearing that a bathing beauty sold for hundreds of dollars, assume these common, poorly done items must be worth the same, charging top quality prices for low quality bathing beauties. While such dealers should not be condemned for their ignorance, a collector must be careful of the old story that "I heard a bathing beauty last week sold for eight hundred dollars, so this one has to be worth at least four hundred, and I'll let you have it for two."

Illustration BS4. 2½in (6cm) tall precolored bisque bathing beauty. Right hand drilled to hold an object (the parasol is a replacement). Incised "Germany" on the back of her legs and "GES. GESCH/Sp. 1608" across the lower back.

Illustration BS5. 3½in (9cm) tall bisque bathing beauty, made to sit on a shelf. Incised "12823" on the right hip.

Illustration BS6. 4in (10cm) tall precolored bisque bathing beauty. Incised on the back of the base "Germany//Sp.432."

For some reason, china bathing beauties do not seem to be as well liked by collectors as their bisque sisters. This seems to mirror the complaints among china doll collectors that German and French bisque dolls are "oohed" and "ahhed" over while their rarer and older china dolls are ignored. Perhaps it is because bisque often copies the warmth and texture of human skin, while china, with its glazed surface, seems cold and artificial. However, there are beautiful china bathing beauties worthy of being included in even the most advanced collections. *Illustration BS10* is an example of an unusual and beautifully executed china bathing beauty. 5in (13cm) long, one of her most striking features is the grace of her long hands. The slender hands, which have free thumbs, index fingers, and little fingers, rival those on the finest figurines. It was necessary to mold both arms separately, adding them at the shoulders, in order to create such lovely hands. She also suns in the most stunning swimsuit. Her cloche bathing cap is black with bright yellow stripes and jaunty bow. The black tunic suit, with its daring deep "V" back, is also trimmed with yellow stripes that match the bathing shorts and strapless slippers. The bathing shorts, while painted almost to her knees, are actually molded to just peek out from under the bathing tunic, but someone appears to have decided that would have been a little too much bare leg for the market. Glossy brown

hair curls against her lightly blushed cheeks and she has black one stroke brows, black eyes completely lined in black, nose dots, and coral beestung lips, all painted with the same attention given to her delicate hands and smart swim attire. Her complexion is even and very pale. There are no marks.

Illustrations BS11 and BS12 are part of the same series. Even if they were not incised "Germany//6779," and "Germany//6781," respectively, their painted, but unmolded, pink swimsuits, glossy dark red-brown hair, and odd light blue slippers with low heels and curled up toes would suggest a family relationship. Both are of nice quality china with good modeling and decoration. *Illustration BS11* has a light blue swimcap with a pink daisy on each side, one stroke brows, black eyes and lid lines, and deep red lips. While her cheeks are blushed, her complexion was otherwise left creamy white. Her left arm was added at the shoulder. She is 5½in (14cm) long.

A half inch shorter than her sister, *Illustration BS12* has a lightly tinted complexion, but no swimcap. Her lips are fuller and more coral, and while her raised left arm appears to have been molded with her torso, the right leg may have been added at the thigh. Together, these two bathers make a delightful pair, but one wonders where is the sister incised "6780"?

(Right)
Illustration BS7. 4in (10cm) tall precolored bisque bathing beauty. Incised on the back of the base "Germany//Sp.433."

(Far Right)
Illustration BS8. 3¼in (10cm) tall precolored bisque figurine. Incised "Germany."

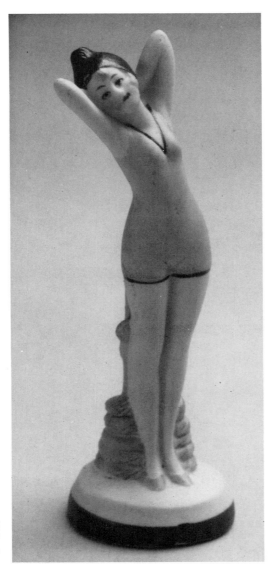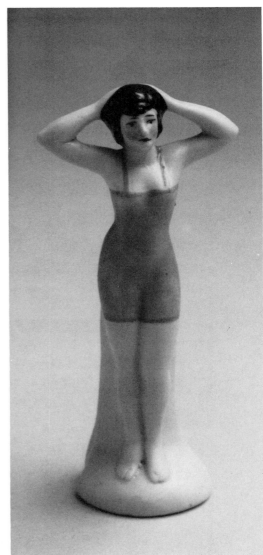

(Below)
Illustration BS9. 3¼in (8cm) long precolored bisque bathing beauty with "snow" on swimsuit and cap. Incised "5684."

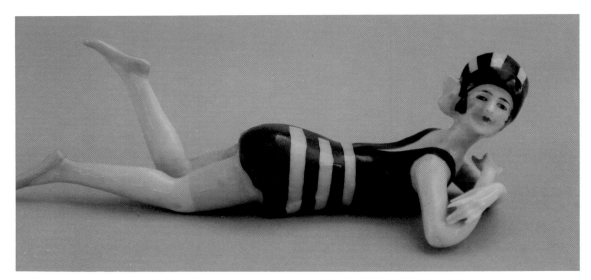

Illustration BS10. 5in (13cm) long china bathing beauty. Unmarked.

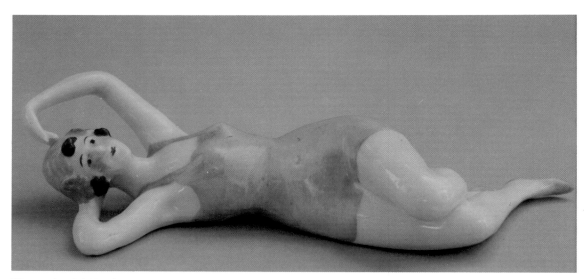

Illustration BS11. 5½in (14cm) long china bathing beauty. Incised "Germany//6779."

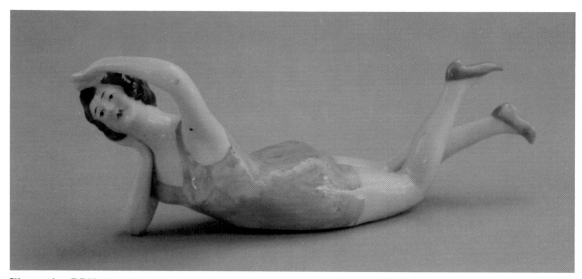

Illustration BS12. 5in (10cm) long china bathing beauty. Incised "Germany//6781."

Mermaids and Sea Nymphs

Mermaids, the finny femmes fatales of the sea, certainly qualify as the most ancient of bathing beauties. For centuries, sailors and fishermen have been terrified, and titillated, by tales of creatures who were beautiful women from the waist up, and cold blooded fish below. Seductive, and without a human soul, the mermaid could lure a ship onto the rocks with her lilting voice or a sailor to a watery death in her arms. To early seafaring peoples she was the metaphor for the sea, on the surface often serene, calm, and lovely, yet capable, without reason or remorse, of plunging men and ships to their deaths in the cold, dark, unknowable waters below. As technology and science eased human fear of the sea, mermaids have been stripped of their murderous mystery and appear in our culture mainly as heroines in sentimental children's stories or decorative pieces for fish tanks. The German manufacturers, and later the Japanese, made the connection between these original sea sirens and their modern bathing suited sisters, and produced mermaids along with their other beach belles.

Illustration M1 shows the more traditional style of mermaid favored by the Germans. The earliest representations of the mermaid in Europe often portrayed her with a split tail, a woman with scaly legs and feet that had changed to fins. This illustration also shows how easily a German manufacturer could make a bathing beauty into a mermaid by simply substituting fins for feet. 3½in (9cm) long, she is of good quality pinkish precolored bisque. Her glossy black bobbed hair (apparently mermaids also followed fashion) is held back by a pale green hairband. The one stroke eyebrows are black, as are the lid lines and dot eyes, and the lips are deep red. Her cheeks are blushed, and her legs pocked with scales from the knees down, ending in twin reddish brown fins. She is rather nicely modeled and decorated, but

is of the simplest construction, needing only a single two part mold. Were she merely a bathing beauty or nudie, she would be nothing special, but as a mermaid she is collectible. German mermaids were apparently made in far fewer numbers than the related bathing beauties and are not frequently found (the Japanese, on the other hand, turned out schools of dumpy bisque and china mermaids for fish tanks). She is incised "Germany" on her back and what appears to be "0399" on the back of her right leg.

The mirthful mermaid of *Illustration M2* is also 3½in (9cm) long, but is a finer specimen. Of tinted bisque, there are openings between her arms and body, and her decoration and modeling are superior. Her very yellow, glossy hair hangs in deeply comb marked curls on her shoulders and down her back, topped with a tiara of brownish flowers. The one stroke brows are dark brown, she has black lid lines and the parted lips are deep red. Her lower legs are covered with light blue scales and she has fins at her calves as well as for feet. She is incised "Germany" in tiny letters underneath and "25186" on the back.

Illustration M3 appears to be the big sister of *Illustration M2*, as she is incised "Germany" underneath in the same tiny letters and "25218" on the back, indicating she is from the same factory and series. 4in (10cm) long, her long light brown hair is topped by a pink daisy. Her one stroke brown brows, black lid lines and eyes, and bee stung bright red lips give her a rather wistful expression. Her light blue scales start at her thighs and she is finned only at the feet. The decoration and modeling are on par with that of *Illustration M2's*.

The Germans did make the half human, half fish version as well, and *Illustration M4* is a most unusual example. Although unmarked, this 5in (13cm) long merperson is

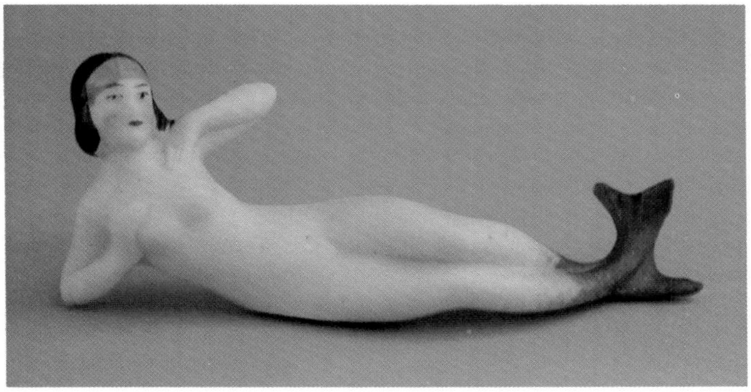

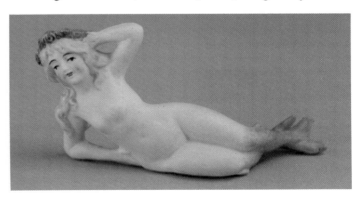

Illustration M1. 3½in (9cm) long precolored bisque mermaid. Incised "Germany" on her back and with what appears to be "0399" on the back of her right leg.

Illustration M2. 3½in (9cm) long bisque mermaid. Incised "25186" on back and "Germany" underneath.

Illustration M3. 4in (10cm) long bisque mermaid. Incised "25218" on the back and "Germany" underneath.

clearly of the best German quality. The cropped orangy hair that appears to hang in damp tendrils on the forehead, the flat chest, and rather broad shoulders make it hard to determine whether this is a merman, mermaid or merchild. Whichever, this is a most unusual item. The outreaching arms, which were added at the shoulders, and cupped hands make it possible for this creature to cling to the side of a goblet or fish globe. The one stroke brows are black, as are the arched lid lines on the goggling eyes and molded donut shaped pupils. The cheeks are puffed, as if distended with water, and the puckered orange-red mouth makes it appear this ocean imp is about to spit a stream at some unsuspecting fish. Although deeply molded scales descend from the waist, the body was left untinted and painted with blue stripes (a favorite decorating technique of William Goebel), as if he or she is wearing a swimsuit. The body terminates into a bright green airbrushed tail. The bisque, like the decoration, is excellent.

Unusually large at 6in (15cm) long, *Illustration M5* is unmarked, but is either of adequate late German or far better than average Japanese quality. Her long light brown hair is entangled with pale green lily pads, and another line of lily pads belt her hips, the sort of nice touches one would expect from a German manufacturer, but which are usually absent on Japanese products. The tinted bisque is of good quality and is far smoother than the coarse bisque usually found in Japanese products. While her one stroke light brown brows, black lid lines, and parted red lips are nicely painted, her rather bulbous nose and orangy blushed cheeks could indicate she is of Japanese origin, as might her rather extraordinary anatomy. Her long, angular arms would hang to her scaly knees, her breasts rise above her armpits, and her elongated torso has deeply indicated ribs and breastbone. While her pale green scales rise as high as her hips, she has the more traditional split tail, which was produced by both

the Germans and Japanese. The decoration is quite good, and if she is Japanese, she indicates they were capable of producing a good competitive product, rather than simply trying to undercut the Germans by flooding the market with crude, cheap copies. Whether Japanese or German, mermaids of this quality are usually not found in such a large size, and the lack of definitive origin does not mar her collectibility.

Although not finned, the next item seems to be a sort of sea nymph. *Illustration M6* appears to be a simple clam shell. 5in (13cm) long, the realistic bisque shell is grayish white with a yellowish wash towards the hinge edge, and is trimmed above the shell's scalloped lips with maroon crescents. However, as shown in *Illustration M7*, lifting the upper shell exposes a dainty nude curled like a pearl within. The applied bisque belle is just 3in (8cm) long, yet her face is beautifully decorated, with dark blonde one stroke brows, red and black lid lines, intaglio black dot eyes, and coral nose dots and lips. Her long blonde hair is straight and faintly brush stroked. While her arms were molded to her body, her legs are free and crossed at the ankles, as if to display her well detailed feet (the upper leg may have been added, but she is so well finished, and so firmly attached to her shell, it is hard to locate the mold lines). By herself, she would be a fine nudie, but with her complete shell (an unknowing dealer or collector, finding her without her upper shell, could reasonably assume she was missing nothing), she is especially collectible. She is incised on the back left edge of the lower shell with the numbers "6641" and on the base with "787", as well as a freehand "39" painted in black.

Illustration M8 also involves a siren and a shell. 5in (13cm) tall, the adolescent figure and bobbed hair of this china figurine (plus the fact she is of rosy pink precolored slip), place her in the twenties. Her short hair is matte black and she has black one stroke brows, pale blue eyes with black lid lines and pupils, and orange-red lips. She was cast separately from the colorful conch shell on which she is seated, so it is possible the same sea nymph could appear on different objects. The realistically modeled shell is painted in fantastic colors; bands of deep blue and orange decorate the shell's lip and crown, while the rest is brushed in orange and green. The quality is high, and far above that of many of the ladies on seashells that were being churned out by Germany and Japan during this period. Underneath she is incised "GERMANY//Sp. 1116," and as theorized in the "By the Sea" chapter, the "Sp." may indicate she is a product of Hertel, Schwab and Company.

Illustration M9 is another lady on the half shell. Such "turtle ladies" must have been popular naughties, as they are found fairly frequently in a number of sizes and in both china and bisque. 3¾in (10cm) long, this typical turtle lady is of bisque. A woman's head and shoulders protrude out of the front of a realistic deep brown turtle shell, while her lower legs poke out through two openings in the rear. Her dark blonde hair is twisted into a topknot. She has dark

blonde one stroke brows, lid lines of the same color, and black dots for eyes. The coral mouth is nicely painted, however, with slightly parted lips and a center lip line. The torso was molded separately and added to the shell, and while it is of good quality oily bisque, the modeling is blurred and the finishing poor. Only the upper section of the shell is decorated, and the even color seems to have been applied with a spray gun (some brownish overspray is visible on the lady's right shoulder). The rather thick legs, of which only the feet are visible from above, have untinted textured stockings and reddish low-heeled pumps. As seen in *Illustration M10*, when the upper portion of the shell is lifted, her back and hips, clad in pale blue undergarments, are revealed. In the more common type, the knickers are open, exposing a bare bottom. However, in this more desirable version, a tiny brown bear is cradled between her legs, its head resting on her buttocks, so she has a "bear bottom." She is incised "GERMANY" underneath.

Illustration M4. 5in (13cm) long bisque mermaid. Unmarked.

Illustration M5. 6in (15cm) long bisque mermaid. Unmarked.

Illustration M6. 5in (13cm) long bisque figurine. Incised on back of lower shell "6641" and underneath with an incised "787" and a free-hand "39" in black.

Illustration M7. View of *Illustration M6* with upper shell removed.

Illustration M8. 5in (13cm) long china figurine.
Incised underneath "GERMANY//Sp. 1116."

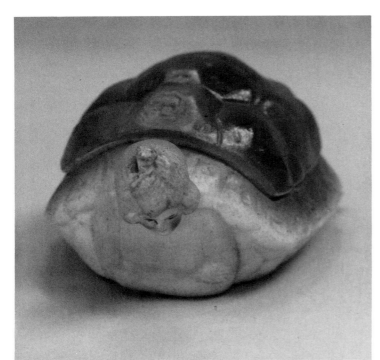

Illustration M9. 3¾in (10cm) long bisque figurine. Incised "Germany" underneath.

Illustration M10. View of *Illustration M9* with upper shell removed.

Naughty, but Nice

When is a lovely lady a bathing beauty and when is she a nudie or a naughtie is a problem discussed throughout this book. Granted, to the collector about to add another exquisite to his or her seraglio, whether she was originally intended to be sold bathing or birthday suited is a minor consideration. Still, for research and catalogue purposes some guidelines are useful. Footwear can provide a clue. For the most part, as set forth in the chapter "Crowning Glory," the wigged bathing beauties wore molded one strap or ballet type bathing slippers. Finding a femme with this type of footwear suggests she could have been sold in a net or lace swimsuit and can be grouped in that genre. Molded heels and sheer stockings are not really suited for beach wear (although I do have one beauty in my collection who wears her original knit swimsuit despite light blue stockings and black pumps), and such a siren may have been intended to be sold nude or in lace lingerie. The pose is also a clue, for the position of the arms or legs may make it impossible to dress a damsel, so that she had to be sold sans swimsuit. I prefer to call ladies with both of these latter two characteristics, or who only possess the last, "nudes" or "nudies," since the intention seems that they were to be sold wearing little more than a come hither look.

Illustration NN1 wears a half mask and a beauty patch, along with long sheer gray stockings and high heeled pumps, generally not considered appropriate beach wear, and her thighs are molded together, so it would have been difficult for her maker to have dressed her. The twenties flirted with fashions of all periods, from the costumes of the French pantomime or the Italian commedia dell'arte to French court dress of the 1700s, Pierrot, Columbine, and La marquise de Pompadour appearing in decorative motifs from prints to pincushion dolls. French fashion artist George Barbier, for example, often portrayed French lovers in the dress of Louis XV, but in the deco style, so that the flavor was of flappers at a costume ball. The half mask and beauty patch recall the elegance, extravagance, and excess of the French court, and perhaps the elite of the 1920s saw some reflection of this era in their own. 5½in (14cm) long, this lady's black mask is molded, although her beauty patch is not. Her blue painted eyes have white irises, perhaps to help them stand out against the mask, as well as black pupils and white highlights. The parted lips are deep orange. Her light gray stockings are untextured and her heeled pumps are a shade darker with black trim and brown soles. Her right arm was added at the shoulder, and her upraised left leg may have been applied at the knee. The white mohair wig is a replacement. She is of excellent bisque and well finished,

but her pale complexion coat has slightly darker splotches that look like a fine layer of dust, indicating some problem in the paint's application or firing. Despite these minor flaws, which can be expected in a mass produced novelty piece manufactured in factories without modern equipment, she is extremely collectible. Illustration MW 207-5200 in *The Collector's Encyclopedia of Half Dolls* shows a bisque pincushion marked with the William Goebel crown and wearing the same mask and beauty patch. The resemblance between the half doll and the whole nudie is so striking that this lounging lady can be attributed to Goebel, despite the fact that she is unmarked.

Illustration NN2, with her crossed legs, also could not have been dressed and was probably meant to be sold as is. 5½in (14cm) long, her light blonde hair is molded in an elaborate quasi-Grecian style, a light blue band in the back holding a wavy chignon in place, while a matching band across her forehead frames curly ringlets. Her one stroke brows match her hair and her painted blue eyes with deep intaglio black pupils have gray and black lid lines. She has coral nose dots and parted lips, which reveal slightly molded teeth. Some artistic license was taken with her long, slim arms, for although they seem proportional, if she could stand, her knuckles would graze her knees. The crossed legs, with their bright pink stockings and black heels, appear to have been applied in one piece. She is incised underneath with a barely legible number that appears to read "5477."

Illustration NN3 has been found in a number of variations, such as with a wig and stockings or with a mask and footwear similar to *Illustration NN1's*. 5in (13cm) tall, her high molded caramel hairdo projects so far back that it was necessary to mold the back of her hair and shoulders separately to avoid undercutting. A turquoise band, with a matching plume and a red jewel set in a golden yellow circle, adorn her hair, which falls in ringlets to her shoulders. She has dark brown one stroke brows and her turquoise eyes are outlined completely in black, with red lid lines and intaglio black pupils. The parted lips are deep coral. The facial features are delicately painted, the bisque is of the best, and her overall rosy complexion is so even (and extends underneath, which usually was left unpainted), her complexion coat may have been done with an airbrush. Her right hand has a free thumb, molded fingernails, and creases in the palm and at the finger joints, while her left holds a green and orange-red rose (the rose's decoration oddly enough does not seem to have been fired and can be scratched off with a fingernail. Underneath, the bisque is the same color as her skin, again suggesting an airbrush was used. If the complex-

Illustration NN1. 5½in (14cm) long bisque figurine. Replaced wig. Unmarked.

ion coat was padded on, the rose would probably have been left uncoated). Her right arm was added at the elbow, the left at the shoulder, and both legs at the hips. Although there is a slight opening between her thighs, she cannot be dressed easily, and in none of the variations I have seen, even though they retained their original wigs, was there any evidence of an outfit. She is stamped "Germany" in black underneath.

Illustration NN4 is of bisque that has had an odd feel, not exactly rough, but as if the bisque was extra porous. When she is held to the light and slowly turned, tiny specks, like grains of crystal or mica, catch the light. One wonders if her manufacturer used a higher portion of feldspar than was usual. 7in (18cm) long, her wavy light brown molded hair is pulled back into a bun. The one stroke brows match her hair, and her painted blue eyes with black lid lines and pupils have mauve eyeshadow. Her deep orange lips are parted and slightly smiling. Although her plump hands seem slightly too small, the rest of her anatomy is beautifully rendered. As seen in *Illustration NN5*, so realistic are her proportions, the picture could almost pass as that of a living nude woman. The complexion, darker than is typical for most nudies, is even, but other examples I have examined have a splotchy appearance, as if this odd feeling bisque had difficulty accepting the color. She has also been seen pure white, with no hint of decoration. Her arms were added at the shoulder and her upper leg at the hip. She is unmarked.

Illustration NN6 has the same crystal specked bisque, mauve eyeshadow, and well rendered anatomy. 5in (13cm)

long, her light brown curly hair is held by a purplish bow, and is puffed into three horizontal tiers of curls in the back. Along with her mauve eyeshadow, she has one stroke brows to match her hair, black lid lines, and gray eyes with slightly intaglio faint black pupils. The small pursed mouth is orange. She appears to be listening attentively to the light green bird with open purple bill that trills on her upraised right hand. The left hand rests by her throat, the free index finger curled in contemplation. Her youthful, taut finger is excellently modeled, but her pale complexion is somewhat deeper colored and orangy between her legs and her arms and torso, as if the color did not fire well and "ran" into the creases, although in this example the unevenness passes as a bit of skillful shading. Both her arms were applied at the elbow. She is unmarked.

Illustration NN7 may also be from the same factory. Although her bisque is not quite as crystalline as *Illustration NN4's* and *NN6's*, it still has the odd porous feel, and she does have mauve eyeshadow. 3in (8cm) tall and long, she twists into a position that demonstrates the sculptor's skill, but does not seem particularly comfortable. Her molded brown hair falls in wings about her face, then is pulled back into a loose bun. She has only black lid lines and large pupils, and her lips are deep orange. Her left arm, which is not visible due to her position, is bent at the elbow, the hand, palm up, almost touching the small of her back, and her right arm stretches across her body to rest just above her left knee. Both hands have free thumbs. The legs cross, but do not

Illustration NN2. 5½in (14cm) long bisque figurine. Incised underneath with a barely legible number that appears to read "5477".

Illustration NN3. 5in (13cm) tall bisque figurine. Stamped "Germany" in black underneath.

touch, and her torso turns slightly to the left, yet she faces straight forward. This complex position required separate molds for her arms and legs, as well as great care and skill in assembling. She is unmarked. Although her pale complexion is even, it has a slightly "off" look, as if the complexion coat was not well absorbed by the bisque or there was some difficulty during firing. In another collection, I have seen three similar ladies in different positions, apparently part of the same series. I have another example in my collection, a studious, but nude, young lady perusing a book, that shares the same odd bisque, mauve eyeshadow, well modeled anatomy, and slightly off complexion coat, and I have seen a birdless, but otherwise near mirror image to *Illustration NN6*. All these unusual characteristics point to one manufacturer, but, as every such lady I have examined is unmarked, there is yet no clue to whom.

Illustration NN8, 4½in (12cm) long, seems to have been part of a popular series of pink bowed ladies. Her dark blonde high piled hair is tied around with a slightly glossy ribbon, a bow on the right side. Her one stroke brows are a shade darker than her hair, and her blue painted eyes have red and black lid lines and black pupils. The coral lips are parted, and all of the facial decoration is delicately painted. She has a flawless, creamy complexion, and although she is very well finished, it appears that her lower leg was applied at the hip. She is unmarked.

Illustration NN9, 3½in (9cm) long, is not simply a smaller version of *Illustration NN8*. She is chunkier, and while *Illustration NN8* arches back, as if to flaunt her slim, sensuous curves, *Illustration NN9* seems to hunch forward, the fold in her abdomen making it look as if she is about to pull in her legs and curl into a ball. Her hands tentatively touch her hair in the back, while *Illustration NN8's* massage her neck, and her legs were molded in one piece. Her blonde hair is comb-marked and the pink ribbon is edged in a darker color. The one stroke brows are also a shade darker than her hair, and her eyes are painted the same as *Illustration NN8's,* but her tiny beestung lips are closed. Although her complexion is well done, it is not as smooth or as peachy as *Illustration NN8's.* She is incised "Germany" on her right back. Is *Illustration NN9* a later or less expensive edition of *Illustration NN8*, or was she a piece by another factory who had no qualms about copying the competition? My feeling is that she is a later piece by the same factory, not only due to similarity in facial featuring and fine decoration, but also because the Germans tended to compete with each other by creating imaginative variations of the same theme, while it was the Japanese who blatantly pirated other designs.

Illustration NN10 is another of the pink bow series. 4in (10cm) long, she is of excellent, slightly oily bisque, with a flawless peachy complexion. Her dark blonde hair is piled atop her head, the bow tied on the left, making her a fine complement to *Illustration NN8 or NN9*. Her one stroke brows match her hair, and her painted blue eyes have red and black lid lines and black pupils. The light coral lips are slightly parted. Her upraised left leg appears to have been applied, but she is so well finished, the mold lines are difficult to trace. She is also incised on her stomach, but the finishing has made it almost illegible. The best that can be made out of is "101//N1". One wonders why, since such care was taken in her finishing, the rather evident air hole under her right arm was not plugged, or at least placed in a less visible location. She has been seen in larger sizes, with her folded arms separate from her bosom. There is also a seated lady of this pink ribboned series and she is the most difficult to find.

Fine quality nudies were also made in china. 4¼in (11cm) tall, *Illustration NN11's* helmet-like hair style and slim angular figure would place her in the mid 1920s. She has caramel colored hair and one stroke brows, and her deeply intaglio blue eyes have black lid lines and large black pupils. The deep orange parted lips have a darker center line and she also has coral nose dots. Her nearly white complexion has faint blushing on her shoulders, down her spine, across her breasts, and on the navel, knees, elbows, fingers, and toes. She is incised underneath her left calf "11896/3" and under her left thigh is stamped in a green circle "MADE IN GERMANY," similar to marks occasionally found on articles from Gerbrüder Heubach. Her short hair, square face, broad shoulders, and adolescent figure give her an androgynous, sensual appeal.

Illustration NN12 has a more feminine beauty. 4¼in (11cm) long, her dark blonde hair is combed back into a high puff. The one stroke brows are a shade darker and she has black dot eyes with extended lid lines, giving her a vampish look. There are coral nose dots and full beestung lips. The graceful hands have free thumbs and the right arm was added at the shoulder. One or both of her slender legs must have been applied, but the mold lines are hidden by the glaze. Her complexion has only the faintest flesh tint. She is incised underneath "6339".

Illustration NN4. 7in
(18cm) long bisque
figurine. Unmarked.

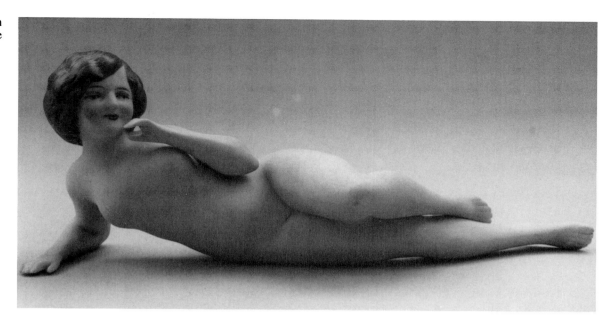

Illustration NN5.
Back view of *Illustration NN4.*

Illustration NN6. 5in
(13cm) long bisque
figurine. Unmarked.

Illustration NN7. 3in (8cm) tall and long bisque figurine. Unmarked.

Illustration NN8. 4½in (12cm) long bisque figurine. Unmarked.

Illustration NN9. 3½in (9cm) long bisque figurine. Incised "Germany" on her back.

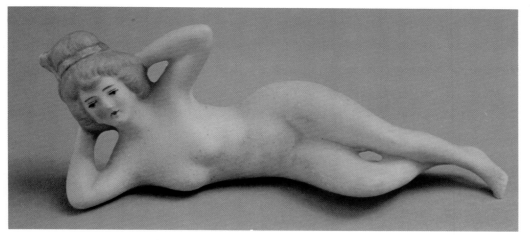

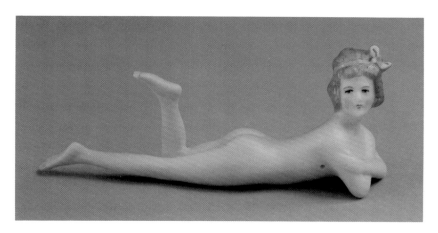

Illustration NN10. 4in (10cm) long bisque figurine. Appears to be incised on stomach "101//N1".

Illustration NN11. 4¼in (11cm) tall china figurine. Incised under the left calf with "11896/3" and under left thigh with a green circle "MADE IN GERMANY."

Illustration NN12. 4¼in (11cm) long china figurine. Incised underneath "6339".

Working Girls

For some bathing beauties, there was more to life than lolling on a beach, or the shelf of a curio cabinet. A number of utilitarian objects, such as pincushions, ashtrays, and vases, were decorated with bathing beauties and nudies. The factories that produced bathing beauties also manufactured pincushion dolls and other knick-knacks, so it was logical and profitable to combine these lines.

Pincushion dolls displaying a full figure are more difficult to find than the typical half dolls, so the collector of bathing beauties and nudies may have to compete with the half doll collectors for these desirable items. *Illustration WG1* is particularly collectible, as she retains her original pincushion. 1¾in (5cm) tall, she is attached to a 1in (3cm) tall pincushion of a silky green material with faint yellow stripes. Of china, she is well modeled and decorated for her size, and demonstrates how a bathing beauty could be transformed into a "useful" pincushion doll by adding a base. Her hair is in a shiny black bob and the one stroke brows are brown. The black dot eyes have black lid lines and the small puckered lips are very red. Her tank suit and slippers are a light red and the tinted complexion is very pale. Because she is securely sewn into the pincushion, it is not possible to fully examine her, but there appear to be no marks. The cloth base of the pincushion, however, is stamped in purple "Made In Germany."

Of such a thin china shell she is translucent when held to the light, *Illustration WG2* is 2½in (6cm) tall. The pale purple scarf covers her hair, except for brown curls around her cheeks. Her yellow tank suit has a purple hem and matching purple slippers. The one stroke brows, large dot eyes, and lid lines are black, and the tiny mouth deep red. Her complexion, except for delicate tinting on her cheeks, was left white. The material, modeling and decoration are of high quality for this type of pincushion doll. She is incised "7405 II//Germany" on the back of her base, which has two sew holes.

Precolored slip was used for china as well as bisque, as in *Illustration WG3*. 2in (5cm) tall, of pinkish precolored china, she wears a light red bathing cap that completely covers her hair, matching tank suit, and slippers. The one stroke brows and lid lines are black, as are the side glancing eyes, and the mouth is merely a red dab. The modeling is very simple and rather blurred, and she was either later, or cheaper, than the preceding pincushion dolls.

Vases were also a popular form of working girl. *Illustration WG4* is an early and beautiful example. 8in (20cm) tall, she is of excellent, translucent, oily bisque. Her light blonde hair is twisted into a complicated braid atop her head and falls in dainty tendrils down her neck. She has dark brown one stroke brows and the blue painted eyes have black pupils and black and red lid lines. Her parted lips, with a darker center line, and nose dots are light coral. She wears a light blue ribbed swimsuit with tarnished gilt trim at the neckline, cuffs, and hem. The slender arms, which were added at the shoulder, end in finely modeled hands with free thumbs, and it appears that a multipart mold was used for the legs and base. The base has two tiers of molded blue waves in the front and the rest, in tones of tan and green, represents a rocky ledge that forms a vase behind her. Although everything about her is of the finest quality, her maker did not seem to think enough of her to mark her. She is incised underneath only "No.183//52" and has a freehand "50" painted in brown.

Although lacking the fine workmanship of *Illustration WG4*, *Illustration WG5* appears to be from the same manufacturer, for the ribbed pattern in her swimwear is the same as her larger sister's. Her blonde hair is a less detailed copy of *Illustration WG4's*, and she has one stroke dark brown brows, black painted eyes with brown lid lines, and a medium coral mouth. Although the facial decoration is nice for this size, the painting on the light blue suit with dark blue trim is sloppy, the blue color sloshing over onto her thighs. She was molded in a single piece, including the blue smear representing water at her feet. Added to the sand colored base behind her is a rather nicely textured tan "wicker" basket with dark brown trim. The finishing was hasty, with evident seams and an opening between her arms that looks as if it were poked through with a dowel. The oily bisque is good and, if a few more minutes had been spent on the production line, she could have been a much finer piece. Marked underneath only with a freehand "13" in dark brown, despite her faults, she is an early item and a nice addition to any collection.

5¾in (15cm) tall, *Illustration WG6* appears to be designed for some useful purpose. Of thin shelled china, the flapper bathing beauty leans on a "rock" base decorated with a spray gun in dark brown and green; the base has a circular opening the size of a nickel in the back, and three smaller holes, one on the right at ankle level, one on her left by her knees, and a third by her right hip. Because the holes are on different levels, she could not have held water, but she could have held pins or perhaps dry or artificial flowers. Whatever her purpose, she is nicely modeled and finished. Her dark brown bobbed hair is covered by a bright orange-red scarf. She has one stroke brown brows, black lid lines and eyes, and bright red beestung lips, all delicately painted.

Illustration WG2. 2½in (6cm) tall china bathing beauty pincushion. Incised on base "7405 II//Germany."

Illustration WG3. 2in (5cm) tall precolored china bathing beauty pincushion. *Private Collection.*

The black tank suit has a white belt and her feet are clad in one strap orange-red bathing slippers. Her clenched right hand is pierced through, and she could have held a dried flower or tiny parasol. Although blurred by the spray gun decoration, the back of her base appears to have been incised "5856//Foreign."

The purpose of *Illustration WG7* is evident. 3¾in (10cm) tall, she is a nipper, meant originally to hold a small amount of liquor. She has a dark blonde bob and matching one stroke brows, black lid lines and pupils, and a coral mouth painted in two parts. Her light blue tank suit has a molded belt and the strapless bathing slippers are a darker blue. The hollow heart and base form the bottle, a small lipped opening in the back closed by a cork. The heart is pierced by a gilt trimmed arrow and decorated by spray gun in orange. The black decal caption on the heart reads "Just a Little Nip," and the gold decal under the heart declares "Souvenir of Hot Springs, Ark." A line of pale green trims the base. She is incised on the back of the base "5581//Germany" and is stamped with red underneath "MADE IN GERMANY." Although a late piece, she is of good quality and is not common.

The type of working girl a collector is most likely to come across is a tank-suited china bather laying on the side of small dish in the shape of a shell or life preserver meant to hold pins or other small items; often the dish portion carries a decal bearing the name of beach or resort the item was a momento of. The quality of these little items is at best adequate and, since they are rather common, they must have been produced in the tens of thousands for souvenir stands all over the country. *Illustration WG8* is a large and better quality example of this genre. 4in (10cm) wide, the scal-loped shell with well modeled ridges is of a pearly, iridescent glaze. The bather was molded separately, except for her left forearm, which was made as part of the shell, so that the same figure could be used on different bases. Her bobbed hair, one stroke brows, lid lines, and dot eyes, are all glossy black, and the bow lips deep red. The tank suit is a deep orange-red and the strapless bathing slippers are black. The painting is acceptable, although hurried, and a black dot was left on the tip of her nose, a rather odd place for a beauty patch. She is unmarked.

The trinket box in *Illustration WG9* is an also fairly common form of working girl. In this china 3½in (9cm) example, the bather was molded separately from the shell, which lifts off, showing that this is literally a box turtle. Like their sisters on the seashells, these are late items and the decorating is often sloppy. The work on *Illustration WG9* is somewhat better than average. Her mottled yellow and red cap just covers her black bobbed hair. The eyes, with their one stroke black brows and dot irises, are completely outlined in black, a detail that would have been far more attractive if they were the same size and on the same level. She does have coral nose dots and the nicely painted beestung lips appear to be smiling. Her tank suit is bright green, trimmed in black, and the green strapless slippers match her suit. The complexion is nice and even, and the finishing well done. The turtle's shell is realistically mottled in dark and light browns, and the turtle itself is airbrushed dark green with yellowish underparts, his features painted in black. Both Germany and Japan churned out these items. She is not marked with a country of origin, but is incised under the turtle only "10302/VIII." The numbers are done in European-style script and the use of Roman numerals also suggests the box is of European, probably German, origin, although she could also be good quality Japanese work.

Useful naughties were also made and *Illustration WG10* is a most appealing example. 5½in (14cm) high, this china item is of a baby falling through a covered pot. The chubby, rosy baby has slightly comb-marked blond hair with a cowlick sticking up and a part on the right side of the head. His (for he looks very boyish) one stroke brows match his hair and the blue painted eyes have red lid lines and black pupils and lid lines. The nostrils are indicated by deep red crescents, and the mouth, open in distress, is light coral with darker red accent lines and center. The fat hands and feet are beautifully molded and the body is lavish with folds and dimples. He has thoughtlessly sat down on a light blue pot covered with a pale yellow "cloth" (the cover is tied down with molded pink twine, which also forms a handle), and the cover is giving way. When the lid is lifted, as seen in *Illustration WG11*, his plump bottom is exposed. There is an opening for a spoon behind the baby, so this item could have been used for some sort of relish or sugar. Despite the excellence of workmanship, it is unmarked except for "4723" incised underneath.

Illustration WG12 is similar in idea, but not quality. 4½in (12cm) tall, this poorly done china trinket box could be either German or Japanese (and since she is unmarked, no one seemed to want to claim her). Her dark blonde bob, one stroke brows, black lid lines and pupils, and orange-red mouth are messily dabbed on and her airbrushed light blue dress runs over onto her pinkish complexion. The ottoman looking base was also done with a spray gun in purple maroon. As seen in *Illustration WG13*, she is hinged to her base by a bit of cheap wire, and when lifted up, exposes not only split knickers and black stocking (long out of date by the time she was made), but her bare buttocks as well. The hole by her left thigh is a factory flaw, but whoever made her cared so little about quality that she was sent out to market anyway. She is not too common, but then, considering the workmanship, it may be just as well. This is the sort of piece that, if it can be picked up inexpensively, serves to round out a collection of naughties, but the collector should not pay a premium price just for black stockings or split knickers. Old fashioned undies do not necessarily mean the piece is early or of good quality.

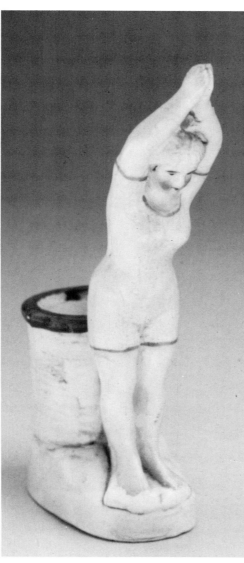

Illustration WG4. 8in (20cm) tall bisque bathing beauty with attached vase. Marked underneath with incised "No. 183//52" and a freehand "50" in brown.

Illustration WG5. 4¾in (12cm) tall bisque bathing beauty attached to molded basket. Marked with a freehand "13" in dark brown underneath.

Illustration WG6. 5¾in (15cm) tall china bathing beauty attached to perforated base. Incised on back of base "5856//Foreign."

Illustration WG7. 3¾in (10cm) tall china bathing beauty "nipper." Caption on heart reads "Just a Little Nip," and gold lettering under heart reads "Souvenir of Hot Springs, Ark." Incised on back of base "5581//Germany" and stamped in red underneath "MADE IN GERMANY."

(Above)
Illustration WG8. 4in (10cm) wide china bathing beauty on shell. Unmarked.

(Left)
Illustration WG9. 3½in (9cm) china trinket box of bathing beauty seated on a turtle. Incised "10302/VIII" underneath the turtle.

Illustration WG10. 5½in (14cm) tall china relish pot or sugar bowl of a baby falling through a covered container. Incised "4723" underneath.

Illustration WG11. Underside of the lid of *Illustration WG10*.

Illustration WG12. 4½in (12cm) tall china trinket box. Unmarked.

Illustration WG13. Underside of lid of *Illustration WG12*.

Thousand and One Nights

The East has long held a fascination for the West. It was a decayed and decadent dreamland of brutal sultans whose word meant life or death, harems where dark eyes glanced out from behind screened windows, slave girls who danced in shimmery veils and tinkling coins, ancient cities encrusted with precious stones, markets dealing in rare spices and Black slaves. Antione Galland's translation of *The Thousand and One Nights* in 1704 engendered a passion for the exotic East, or at least as Westerners imagined it. Eastern themes began to appear in art from painting to opera. Harem scenes of nude or barely draped women, as ripe as fruit and as lustrous as pearls, became an acceptable form of voyeurism, though often such paintings were nothing more than a European model sprawled over Oriental rugs and adorned with paste jewels. And, for the West, the East was like these imagined harem slaves, passionate, frivolous, languorous, exotic, and waiting to be conquered by the more virile and purposeful Europeans. By the mid 1800s, the East was becoming more accessible to Western tourists, both the wealthy elite and growing middle class coming to sail the Nile or peer at the Pyramids. Orientalism in art and decoration promised an imagined escape from the proprieties of Victorian life. This trend continued through the turn of the century, with the printing of a new translation of *The Thousand and One Nights* by Dr. Joseph-Charles Mardus. Mata Hari, the "Eye of Dawn" (actually Marguertha Geertruida Zelle, the daughter of a middle class Dutch family), first danced in Paris in 1905. The 1907 premier of Richard Strauss' "Salome" at New York's Metropolitan Opera shocked patrons with Salome's seductive and serpentine dance that ended with her kissing the head of John the Baptist. Although the opera was withdrawn after that single performance, it inspired a generation of Salome dancers, from artistes such as Ruth St. Denis to the less lofty stage of the Zeigfeld Follies. Colette also shocked the allegedly more sophisticated French the same year when she danced the part of an Egyptian mummy reanimated by a European scholar in "Rêve d' Egyptien" at the Moulin Rouge, unraveling yards of wrapping to reveal a scantily clad seductress and ending with a passionate kiss on the lips of the scholar, played by a woman in male garb. Sergei Diaghilev's Ballets Russe performed "Cleopatra" in 1909 and "Scheherazade" in 1910, Russian artist Leon Bakst costuming the sultanas and slaves in brilliant, bold colors and swirling fabrics. And, as discussed in the chapter entitled "From Victoria to Vamp," Paul Poiret set about dressing the fashionable Edwardian female as a would be odalisque. The 1920s thrilled to the romance of the film

"The Sheik" in 1921, which spawned not only its own sequel, but numerous imitators, and the discovery of Tutankhamun's tomb in 1922 heralded Egyptian influenced clothing, jewelry, and accessories. The German bisque manufacturers did not pass up their chance to cash in on this fascination with the exotic East and, along side the bathing beauties, produced harem ladies and belly dancers.

Illustration H1 is an excellent example of how the East influenced Western fashion. 4½in (12cm) high, this fine figurine could have been dressed by Poiret himself. Her dark blonde hair, which is pulled back into a low chignon, is adorned with a pink headpiece sporting an aigrette of real black plumes. Her outfit consists of a short sleeved tan tunic gathered at the hips with a square décolleté neck filled in with lace. The draped underskirt is deep green and both the tunic and skirt are decorated with pinkish glitter. Her long gloves and lone slipper peeking out from the skirt are mint green. Such a neckline came into fashion in 1911, and the lavish tunic and long skirt fell out of favor during World War I, so she probably dates to around 1913. The bisque, modeling, and decoration are of the highest quality in this Edwardian beauty. Her blonde one stroke brows match her hair, the painted blue eyes have black lid lines and pupils, there are coral nose dots, and her parted deep coral lips trace a slight smile. Except for a freehand "30" painted underneath in black, she is unmarked.

Illustration H2 demonstrates how easily a standard bathing beauty could be transformed into a light of the harem. 4¾in (12cm) long, this sultana is of good quality precolored bisque with fired features. She is well decorated for this type, with dabs of black bobbed hair peeking out from beneath her headdress, light brown one stroke brows, blue painted eyes with black lid lines and pupils, and full coral lips. Her right arm was added just beneath the shoulder, and possibly (it is hard to tell through her harem pants) her upraised right leg was added as well. Although her yellow turban-like cloche with its green medallion looks very Middle Eastern, such head wear was the standard for the 1920s. Her yellow and green bra, dotted with red, is not molded, but merely painted on and fired. She is dressed as found, and her costume is old and beautifully sewn. The girdle is of red silk trimmed in yellow and her billowy yellow harem pants are of (sadly melting) silk crepe. The red and clear bead bracelets on her ankles and right wrist are also old. The dark green painted slippers add to her Eastern look, yet are the same as found on many bathing beauties of the period. This model has been seen sans bra, beads, and harem pants, and passes as a typical bathing beauty. Perhaps

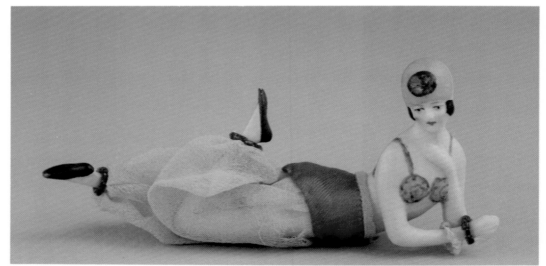

Illustration H2. 4¾in (12cm) long precolored bisque figurine wearing old silk harem pants. No visible marks.

Illustration H3. 4½in (12cm) tall bisque figurine with original wig. Incised "852" under right hip and "F.X." under left.

Illustration H4. Closeup of *Illustration H3's* face.

Illustration H5. 7½in (19cm) tall bisque nodder representing interpretive dancer Maud Allan.

some jobber special ordered a standard bathing beauty, adding the bangles and painted bra with the idea of cashing in on the 1920s' fascination with sheiks and their swooning captives.

4½in (12cm) high, *Illustration H3* strikes a stereotypical pose of a harem dancer. Her brown mohair wig with its elaborate headpiece appears original (the same model with a similar wig and headpiece is illustrated in Plate MW 937-401 of *The Collector's Encyclopedia of Half Dolls*, and still retains the melting remains of her silk harem outfit). The comma shaped hair ornament is of wire covered with brown rick-rack and filled in with mesh, onto which is sewn blue faceted stones, a cluster of faux pearls, and four long strands of silvery beads that fall to her breast. The face is decorated in a manner similar to the finest bathing beauties, with brown one stroke brows, red lid lines, and eyes outlined completely in black. Her slightly intaglio eyes are brown, instead of the more usual blue (perhaps in tribute to the fact she is supposed to be Middle Eastern), and the full lips an orangy red. The bisque is excellent, and her skin is a pale olive tone. Around her narrow waist is a white molded belt or loin cloth decorated with raised blue and red jewels (but only in the front. Although the jewels are molded throughout, they were left unpainted in the back). The elongated hands have free thumbs and a bracelet of tarnished metal adorns her right wrist. Beneath her right hip she is incised "852" and "F.X." under her left hip. In the section on

Illustration H6. Old postcard of 1908 study of Allan by Reutlinger.

Illustration H7. Postcard with portrait of Allan postmarked September 29, 1908.

William Goebel under the chapter "Ladies With A Past," *Illustrations G10, G11, and G12* are all incised with an "F" followed by another letter, and based on this, and the superb quality of this figurine, she can be attributed to Goebel as well. *Illustration H4* is a closeup of her face and displays the fantastic quality of decoration.

Illustration H5 is not just a rare nodder, she is also a celebrity. 7½in (19cm) tall, this bisque belly dancer is meant to represent Maud Allan, the Canadian born interpretative dancer who enthralled Europe in the early 1900s with her grace and scanty costumes. She was best known for her interpretation of the title role in "The Vision of Salome". *Illustration H6* is a postcard of the 1908 photograph of Allan by Reutlinger, who photographed so many turn of the century belles of the hour. The figurine and the postcard display identical costumes, even to the bracelets and rings, but the pose is slightly different, for in the figurine the arms are moved before the face, instead of over the head. The reason for this alteration is to allow movement of the head which, on a wire strung through the forehead, nods gently from side to side. Her torso is also a separate piece, strung on a wire that pierces the hollow skirt from front to back, and sways when gently tapped. The torso fits over a long clapper that reaches almost the base of the hollow lower portion. The clapper was made separately from the torso and they were joined with slip at the greenware stage and fired

together; the figurine cannot be disassembled, as the clapper is too wide to pull up through the waist and the torso, with its upraised arms, cannot be pulled down through the skirt. The idea and execution are exquisite, and she was a complex piece to manufacture and assemble. The bisque is sharp and the modeling surprisingly intricate, although the decoration skims over much of the molded details. Her hair is a short black bob, and her headpiece is picked out in dull gold, with a red jewel above her forehead. The one stroke brows are dark brown and her deeply molded eyes have dark brown lid lines and black pupils. Her full pouting lips are deep coral. The facial features closely resemble the portrait of Allan that appears on the postcard, postmarked September 29, 1908, in *Illustration H7*. The beading on the molded bra exactly duplicates the costume worn by Allan in the Reutlinger photograph, but in the figurine it is only lightly decorated in an odd pinkish color, the red jewels on the breastplates and belly decoration faintly indicated. The coloration is even paler on the belt which hangs over the light taupe skirt, and neither the belt or bra are decorated in the back, although the molded details are there. One wonders why, when presented with this elaborate and exotic costume, the decorator chose such pale and dull colors. Allan stands on a light green base and is unmarked, so the manufacturer of this delightful dancing tribute is unknown.

Ladies with a Past

While today's collector may admire the elegance and artistry of bathing beauties and nudies, apparently their manufacturers were not so enamored. After all, these little figurines were, to their makers, just a small sideline to cash in on a current fad. Not only did their small size and design often leave little space for a mark, there was no incentive for a manufacturer to do so. However, for a collector sensitive to family resemblances, the rare marked figurine or an old company catalogue page or an advertisement can provide clues as to who might be the manufacturer of a certain little lady. Without a definite mark, any such guess, no matter how educated, is best categorized as an attribution. This chapter discusses the marked, and attributed, products of the firms of: Dressel, Kister and Company; Galluba and Hofmann; William Goebel; Alfred Pensky; and, Schafer and Vater. While Dressel, Goebel, and Schafer and Vater did often mark their products, the sections concerning the other companies are attributions based on my best educated guesses. I describe in some detail the reasons and research on which I base my speculations, and the reader is invited to disagree. As the popularity of naughties, nudies, and bathing beauties grow, no doubt more marked figurines and other clues will be discovered and shared among collectors.

Dressel, Kister and Company

Dressel, Kister and Company is another manufacturer familiar to doll collectors for its extremely beautiful and elegant pincushion and china dolls. Like other companies, such as that of William Goebel, it also produced ladies, lovely nudes of bisque and creamy china. Also, like William Goebel, Dressel proudly marked many of its products. Founded in 1837 by Freidrich Kister, it offered doll heads and "tea-cosy dolls" as late as 1949. However, it is safe to assume most of the nudies produced by this long lived company were created when the demand was greatest for such figurines, from the beginning of this century through the early 1930s.

Illustration DK1 may be familiar to collectors of half dolls, as she is the full figured sister of a sought after Dressel pincushion belonging to its medieval series (the pincushion doll is pictured in Illustration MW107-520 of *The Collector's Encyclopedia of Half Dolls*). 4in (10cm) long, she is of pale precolored slip, and has a soft, luminous glaze. Her dark gray hair is braided into two loops that cover her ears and meet in the back in a bun beneath her gold headband with raised turquoise dots. Her tresses are delineated by thin white streaks, looking as if they were carefully scratched through the darker gray, giving her hair a deeply comb-marked appearance. The gray hair seems incongruous on this nubile nude, but it was a favored hair color of Dressel. Her face is carefully decorated, with one stroke dark gray brows, red and black lid lines, brown eyes with black pupils (unlike the rest of the bisque and china world, Dressel appears to have loved dark eyed ladies, and brown eyes predominate in its products), red nose dots and beestung lips, and softly blushed cheeks. Her modeling, from the muscles in her back to her slender toes, is of the highest quality. She has been found in larger sizes, and in these bigger pieces the facial painting is more elaborate, the eyes ringed by gray. Dressel does seem to have had a problem with slag, and while this piece is blemish free, I have seen a number of nudes marred by unsightly speckles in their backs and bottoms. She is marked underneath with a Dressel mark, looking something like a spiky reverse question mark in dark blue; she is also stamped in a lighter blue with a cursive "Germany" and a figure "8".

Illustration DK2 has the streaked gray hair and brown eyes characteristic of Dressel. She also shows the connection between these figurines and the pincushion dolls. 2¼in (3cm) high when removed from her wood stand, she sits upon a small tapering unglazed base, like a pincushion doll's, except it is solid and there are no sew holes. This odd base is also evidence the old wood stand may be original, as not only does she screw neatly into it with a perfect fit, she cannot sit up without its support. Dressel sometimes provided elaborate bases for its pincushion dolls and also produced standing and dancing nudes who were supported by a wooden base with a metal rod that fit into a hole through the sole of a foot, which further suggests this wood stand is original. Her gray hair is pulled into a low chignon and her facial decoration is in the same colors and of the same high quality as *Illustration DK1's*. She has also been found in larger sizes without the molded base and the wood stand. Of pale precolored slip, she has the same excellent modeling and soft glow as found in *Illustration DK1*. She is marked on her molded base with the blue Dressel question mark and the figure "8".

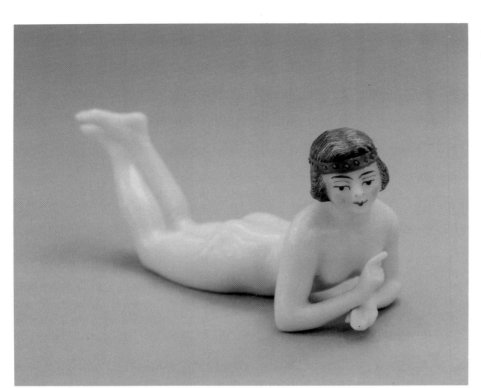

4in (10cm) long china figurine. Marked in light blue with "Germany" in cursive and "8", and "🕭" in darker blue.

Illustration DK2. 2¼in (3cm) tall china figurine. Marked in blue on the base with "🕭" and "8".

Galluba and Hofmann

Established by Hugo Galluba and Georg Hofmann in 1891, this firm, like so many of its German counterparts, included bathing beauties, pincushions, and bisque ladies among its products. In 1910, Galluba and Hofmann advertised "Multi-colored painted and dressed porcelain figures." These were wigged bisque figurines of women and children dressed in elegant and fashionable clothing of real fabric, including a line inspired by the fancy dress ball costumes of the Monte Carlo flower carnival. The figurines could be purchased either attached to a bisque pedestal or a candy box. In Germany, to protect a design from imitation, a factory could register the model number with the District Court, obtaining a geschmachsmunster or "G.M." In doll manufacturing, this registered factory number is identical to the mold number, and even when the maker is unknown, if the G.M. registration for the mold number can be located, it can lead the researcher back to the manufacturer. In this same year, Galluba and Hofmann registered a 400 series of G.M. numbers, from 400a through 410. In 1914, they introduced another series of 400 numbers for their "Vienna style fashion dolls." Although Galluba died in 1916,

Hofmann, and co-owner Kommerzienrat Alfred Teufel, advertised bathing beauties in outfits of silk net and pincushion dolls as late as 1930.

A page from the 1914 catalogue shows a bevy of beauties, several with a child, in luxurious Edwardian garb (except for a single male and female pair in what appears to be French court dress of the time of Marie Antoinette). All of the figurines are standing in elegant poses, and appear to be supported by either a molded pedestal or are posed against a decorative pillar. Their long slim arms are free from the body, and their perfect oval faces are supported on necks that seem too slender, especially in proportion to these dainty ladies' surprisingly wide shoulders. The luscious costumes appear to be made of real laces, silks, and feathers, and many of the models wear a distinctive mohair wig with a center seam that is puffed into "wings" on each side. The footwear, on the other hand, appears molded, and the ladies all stand with one toe fashionably pointed forward. The model numbers range from 400 through 414, often followed by letter.

(Right)
Illustration GH1.
5½in (17cm) tall bisque figurine. Incised "405" at base of pedestal.

(Far Right)
Illustration GH2.
3in (8cm) tall bisque pincushion. Incised "5693" on back.

Illustration GH3. Closeup of *Illustration GH2's* face.

Illustration GH1 shares a number of characteristics that suggest she is from Galluba. 5½in (17cm) tall, she is marked "405" at the base of her pedestal, and both her pedestal and one foot forward pose mirror the ladies in Galluba's catalogue. The base of the pedestal is hollow and filled with a plaster type substance with a broken off metal pin in the center. This would have enabled the manufacturer to attach her to a variety of bases, such as Galluba advertised. Although her wig is a replacement, her oval face, too slim neck, and over broad shoulders also suggest Galluba. Despite her disproportionate anatomy, she is still lovely. Her one stroke brows are dark brown and her slightly intaglio eyes have red lid lines, black upper and lower lid lines, white highlights, and a dark ring around the blue iris. Her full bowed lips and nose dots are pale coral. She holds a molded letter in her graceful hands, which she appears to be glancing at with some disdain (perhaps a plea from a rejected lover?). Her ribbed molded undergarment contains a figure that would have been the envy of any Gibson girl, with its full bosom thrust forward, tiny waist, and ample rump pushed well back over the hips. There is molded eyelet at her knees, the ribbed stockings are pale yellow, and her narrow pumps dark gold. The bisque and decoration are of the highest quality. Her arms and head were added, so a number of poses could be achieved by placing different arms and head on the same basic torso.

Illustration GH2 is clearly *Illustration GH1* adapted into a pincushion top. She wears her original light brown mohair wig puffed into the distinctive winged style seen on the beauties in Galluba's catalogue. Although she shares the same superb quality of decoration and bisque as *Illustration GH1*, her complexion is rosier and her larger pupils give her a more alert look. Her lips are fuller and a deeper shade of coral. There are four sew holes in her base and she is marked "5693." on the back. *Illustration GH3* is a closeup, showing the amazing detail of the face of this 3in (8cm) tall half doll.

Illustration GH4, at least from the shoulders down, has the identical pose and clothing as *Illustration GH1*. 4½in (12cm) tall, not including her base, she demonstrates how a different head and arms could be added to a basic torso to create new models. She is incised "407" followed by a cursive "D" and has the same oval face, slim neck, and wide shoulders as the suspected Gallubas in *Illustrations GH1 and GH2*, although these characteristics are not as pronounced in her smaller size. Her one stroke brows are deep brown and blue painted eyes have only upper red and black lid lines. She has pale coral nose dots and her lips of the same shade are parted in a slight smile. The left hand has a free index finger and thumb and her cupped right hand has a free thumb. Her pedestal is fastened by what feels to be a piece of wire to the top of a small round box (the box long missing) covered in faded tan brocade edged in beige and gold rickrack. Her wig is a replacement.

8½in (22cm) tall, *Illustration GH5* is a large, lovely bathing beauty that may have also come from Galluba. Again there is the oval face, slender neck, and wide shoulders, as well as a family resemblance in her facial features. She stands against a brown bisque "wooden" pier incised "423", followed by a cursive "G". Her ash blonde wig is a long thin coil of mohair that was formed into waves and glued directly to her head, and while both the mohair and glue are old, it is hard to say whether the wig is original. Her one stroke brows are black and her intaglio blue eyes have red lid lines, black upper and lower lid lines, and white highlights. The nose dots and shapely lips are coral. She wears the deteriorating remains of a pink net swim suit and her rather awkward posture, upper torso pushed forward and hips thrust back, reflects the S-shaped figure sculpted by the Gibson girl's corset. Her large graceful hands have free thumbs and molded fingernails and her feet are bare, somewhat unusual as most bathing beauties wear molded slippers. She appears to have been fastened to the gray bisque stand with some sort of plaster at the base of the supporting pier, and perhaps she could be ordered on a variety of bases. The base itself is stamped "Germany" in purple underneath. As with all the preceding suspected Gallubas, her bisque and decoration are of the highest quality. *Illustration GH6* shows the detail of her lovely face.

Illustration GH7 is another beautiful bather that may be from Galluba. 6¼in (16cm) tall, she demonstrates how the bisque figurine was molded separately and could be fastened on different types of bases. Her mohair wig is dark brown, as are her one stroke brows. Her blue painted eyes have red lid lines, black upper and lower lid lines and white highlights. She has coral nose dots and parted lips of the same color. Her apparently original swimsuit is of gold lace trimmed with pale green ribbon. She is supported by a molded clump of tall grass and wears pink ballet type bathing slippers. The base is glued to a piece of cardboard covered in red fabric and she is further supported by a piece of wire tied to her waist, but this arrangement is not original. She could have been easily pegged to a bisque base or the top of a candy box. She is incised on the back of her leafy base "408E", another clue she many be Galluba.

Illustration GH8 may be yet another Galluba bathing beauty. 4½in (12cm) tall, she is on a round grayish stand similar to that in *Illustration GH5*. She retains her original dark brown mohair wig and the melting remains of her silk net swimsuit. Her one stroke brows are dark brown and her painted blue eyes have red lid lines, heavy black upper and lower lid lines, and white highlights. The full heartshaped mouth and nose dots are deep red. She stands against a low "wooden" fence and appears to be pegged to the gray stand. Blue ballet type slippers grace her well turned ankles. She appears to be incised "407" followed by a cursive "M" at the base of the fencepost.

Illustration GH9 is a dainty pincushion on what appears to be her original wire and crepe paper base. 2in (5cm) tall on a 4in (10cm) tall base, she holds one hand to her lips, a pose that seemed to be a favorite of Galluba's (*Illustrations GH4, GH5 and GH7* also strike similar delicate and feminine poses). She retains her original medium brown mohair wig with its puffed wings. Her one stroke brows are dark brown and her eye treatment is similar to *Illustration GH1's*, even to the dark circle around the iris. She has coral nose dots and slightly parted lips. Again, there are the oval head, overly slim neck, and wide shoulders. The right hand has a free thumb and in her left is the fragment of a bisque envelope. Her torso tapers to a narrow waist with four sew holes, and there are curved openings under each arm. She is incised "5694" followed by a cursive "g". *Illustration GH10* reveals the fantastic detail of her tiny face. *Illustration GH2*, another attributed Galluba pincushion doll, is incised "5693". In *The Collector's Encyclopedia of Half Dolls*, there is a pincushion doll that shares the Galluba characteristics of slender neck and contrasting wide shoulders; incised "5690", Illustration MW508-403 is of a delightful young lady with a bright smile, a molded gold and turquoise necklace, and clutching a molded green book. As all of these pincushions share the Galluba family traits and are all incised with a four digit number beginning with "569", this may have been Galluba's series for pincushion dolls.

Illustration GH4. 4½in (12cm) tall bisque figurine. Incised on base of pedestal "407D".

Illustration GH5. 8½in (22cm) tall bisque figurine wearing original swimsuit and old mohair wig. Incised "423G".

Illustration GH6. Closeup of *Illustration GH5's* face.

Illustration GH7. 6¼in (16cm) tall bisque figurine, wearing original swimsuit and wig. Incised "408E" on base. *Private Collection.*

Illustration GH8. 4½in (12cm) tall bisque figurine with original swimsuit and wig. Incised "407M" on base. *Private Collection.*

(Below Left)
Illustration GH9. 2in (5cm) tall bisque pincushion on 4in (10cm) wire and crepe paper base. Original wig. Incised "5694g".

(Below Right)
Illustration GH10. Closeup of *Illustration GH9's* face.

William Goebel

The factory of Franz Detlef Goebel and his son, William Goebel, is well known to collectors of dolls and half dolls, but, like many other German porcelain factories, Goebel also produced bathing beauties. Goebel appears to have marked a number of its bathing beauties and related items, for its bisque ladies are the only ones that appear with a maker's mark with any frequency. Perhaps Goebel marked its products out of well earned pride, for those carrying the Goebel mark tend to be of the highest quality.

The 6½in (17cm) long voluptuous nude in *Illustration G1* is not marked, but she is a treasure not only because of her size and beauty, but also because she was purchased from the daughter of her original owner. Known as "Daddy's doll," according to the woman who sold her, the full-figured figurine lay on a white fur "rug" in her mother's curio cabinet for many years. Her parents were married in 1904, her sister was born in 1906, she in 1914, and she and her sister recall "Daddy's doll" from their earliest years; in fact, the woman wondered if the figurine might be a souvenir from Daddy's bachelor days. The figurine can be safely dated around the 1910s and may even predate 1904. Of smooth creamy bisque, her ample curves are lavishly blushed and her fair complexion is flawless. Her dark blonde molded hair is caught by a pale blue fillet in a quasi-Grecian style, the hair waving back from her full face and gathered at the nape of her neck in a loosely braided bun. The one stroke brows match her hair and her slightly intaglio blue eyes have red and black lid lines. Her deep coral lips turn up in a slight alluring, smile, one delicate finger motioning some fortunate viewer closer. The graceful hands are beautifully modeled, even to the fingernails, and such delicate detail would have added to the time and expense of production. Both arms were molded separately and added at the shoul-

ders, and the upbent leg was also added. The artistry and expertise such a figurine required in the sculpting, molding, assembling, and decorating indicate that even in her day she was probably a fairly expensive decorative piece. *Illustration G2* shows the detail of her face.

Illustration G3, while sharing the same ample anatomy, beautiful complexion, and classical hairstyle, is seated, pensively smiling as she leans forward, a rose beneath one supporting hand. 4¼in (11cm) tall, both her arms and legs appear to have been added. Although unmarked, she is undoubtedly from the same factory as *Illustration G1*.

And just who that factory belonged to is suggested by *Illustration G4*. 5in (13cm) long, this reclining nude shares the same creamy bisque, lush blushing, and fleshy contours as the preceding figurines. The hair is the same color and in a similar Grecian influenced style, only there is an additional band across the back of her head. Her facial features are less detailed and she has only black lid lines and pupils. She came reclining on what was said to be her original fur rug, and it is clear she and the now yellowed scrap of fur have been together for many years, as it carries the deep permanent impression of her body. Could this be similar to the long discarded fur rug that *Illustration G1* once rested on? A smaller and less complicated piece, only the left arm, which shades her eyes, was added at the shoulder. Her most important feature is that she is clearly marked with the crown and intertwined "G" and "W" of William Goebel. The crown was first used around 1900, so she postdates the turn of this century. The incised numbers accompanying the marks are not as clear, but appear to be "99//8H/1".

At one doll show, I saw a slightly smaller variation of *Illustration G1*. There were the same features and coloring, but she had her arms molded against her chest, her blonde

Illustration G1. 6½in (17cm) long bisque figurine. Unmarked.

Illustration G2. Closeup of *Illustration G1.*

Illustration G3. 4½in (11cm) tall bisque figurine. Unmarked. *Private Collection.*

hair tucked into a blue and white polka dot sun bonnet topped by a pink bow, and she was wearing a jaunty blue and white striped swimsuit and deep maroon slippers. Unfortunately I hesitated, and she was lost to a more decisive collector. However, soon after, I came across *Illustration G5*, who is dressed in the same stylish swimwear. Clearly she is a dressed version of *Illustration G4*. 5in (13cm) long, her blue and white swimsuit is not merely painted on, as "fabric" is indicated by wrinkles and the little light blue bows on her straps are molded. In fact, the blue in her straps and bonnet match that in the hair ribbons of *Illustrations G1 through G4* and she shares the same features and coloring. Her strapless slippers are a deep maroon. She lies on a tiny terry cloth towel trimmed in deep red, and alleged to be original. The towel has aged to gray, except for where her rounded body rested, so she has lain there for many years. Other than "Germany" stamped in black under her right thigh, she is unmarked, but is surely from Goebel. As in *Illustration G4*, her left arm was molded separately and added.

Illustration G1 was said to have lain on a piece of white fur, discarded after it became yellowed and worn. *Illustra-*

tion G4 came with what was alleged to be her original fur rug, while *Illustration G5* was accompanied by a miniature towel, and both figurines had certainly reclined on their respective accessories for many years. Are these accessories original? While admittedly it could be coincidence that these three beauties came with, or were said once to have had, a rug or towel, the fact they were all made by the same factory, and probably during the same period of time, certainly gives force to the argument that the accessories are original. Did Goebel decide that supplying its figurines with appropriate miniature props would give it an edge over its competitors, who were also attempting to profit from the bathing beauty craze? Or were the accompanying articles added by some middle party who hoped that supplying these inexpensive bits of fur and cloth would increase the figurines' appeal to the consumer?

Illustration G6 is yet another variation of *Illustrations G4 and G5*. 4in (10cm) long, her striped swimsuit is red and white and she wears a chic pink turban topped by a white plume. Her slippers are the same deep maroon as *Illustration G5's*, but the straps were added sometime in her past by someone seeking to disguise a break in her left foot. Her left

68

Illustration G4. 5in (13cm) long bisque figurine on fur rug. Incised "99 8H//1", Goebel crown, and intertwined "G" and "W".

Illustration G5. 5in (13cm) long bisque figurine on miniature towel. Stamped "Germany."

Illustration G6. 4in (10cm) long bisque figurine. Unmarked.

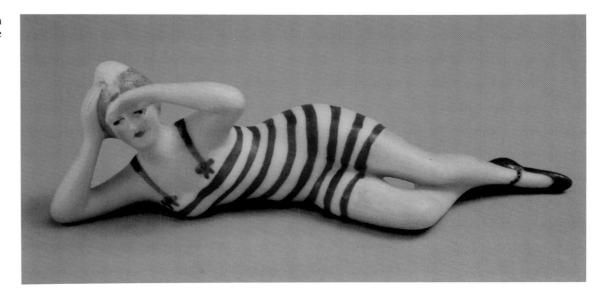

arm, as in *Illustrations G4 and G5*, was added at the greenware stage, but unlike them, she has red and black lid lines and painted blue eyes.

Illustrations G7 and G8 are larger versions of *Illustrations G5 and G6*. 6in (15cm) and 5in (13cm) long, respectively, their larger size allows for more detail. The facial features of *Illustration G7* closely resemble those of *Illustration G1*, even to the subtle sly smile, and *Illustration G8* carries a slight hint of that smile. Her coloring is similar to that of *Illustration G6*, except that her turban is light blue. *Illustration G7* is incised underneath with a line of figures and letters. "H 901/1", and carries the faint stamp "Bavaria." The incised marks on *Illustration G8* are not legible, but she is stamped in black "Bavaria."

While all these figurines postdate the beginning of this century, their quality suggests they did not follow too long thereafter. *Illustration G9* is a postcard sent by a gentleman in Ogden, Utah, on October 18, 1907, to a male acquaintance in Peabody, Kansas. The two models, who seem rather skeptical about the fish they have "caught," wear striped swimsuits, one red and white, the other now faded blue and white, that match the painted suits of *Illustrations G5, G6, G7, and G8*. While German manufacturers were loathe to discard costly molds simply to follow the whims of fashion, and often produced a doll or figurine long after her hairstyle or costume had fallen out of favor, the postcard does suggest that these figurines date somewhere around the late 1900s or

early teens. This also supports the story that accompanied *Illustration G1*, which dates her to this period.

Illustration G10 has modestly covered her black bobbed hair with a deep blue scarf and tucked her feet into deep maroon slippers, yet has neglected to slip on a bathing suit. 8in (20cm) tall, she is fastened at the hip to the green vase that serves as her base, so it would have been difficult to dress her. But then, it would have been a shame to hide her graceful form. More athletically built than the previous bathers, she reflects the slimmer figure that became the fashionable silhouette beginning in 1910 and reached the flat-chested hipless extreme in the mid 1920s. Her one stroke brows are brown, the blue painted eyes have red and black lid lines, and the deep red lips are slightly parted. The slender arms were added at the shoulder and she stands on a green two tier platform that extends up to a narrow bud vase behind her. She is not only lovely, she is also marked. Underneath she is incised "F.N.//760//Dep" above the Goebel crown and intertwined "G" and "W", and is also stamped in black "Germany."

Illustration G11 is also marked. 8in (20cm) tall, she is incised underneath her seat "F.V.//02/1" over the crown mark and intertwined "G" and "W". Her bald pate is covered by an old wig made of red-gold mohair and her one stroke brows are dark brown. The brown eyes have black pupils with white highlights, brown lid lines beneath the eyes emphasizing her laughing expression, and tiny lashes on the

Illustration G7. 6in (15cm) long bisque figurine. Incised "H 901/1" and stamped "Bavaria."

Illustration G8. 5in (13cm) long bisque figurine. Marks illegible.

lower lid (a detail sometimes found on Goebel pincushion dolls), and her coral lips are parted in a deeply molded smile. She wears an elaborate molded white corset with eyelet at the bosom, a blue bow between her breasts, and lacing running all the way down her back, as well as a pair of ruffled knickers. Her feet are adorned with maroon ballet type slippers (maroon seems to have been Goebel's favorite color for footwear). Her seat is flat, enabling her to sit on a shelf edge, but there is a molded channel running from hip to hip, so she could be tied to a pincushion. The cushion she sits on is not original, for under the old tapestry material is a plastic box. A similar figurine, in apparently original condition, seen in another collection sat on an old miniature armchair made of fabric covered pasteboard, which again suggests Goebel may have accessorized its products. *Illustration G11's* head was added, as were her elongated arms and legs, and her dainty hands have free thumbs. Perhaps not as conventionally pretty as her preceding Goebel sisters, she certainly has character and is extremely collectible.

Illustration G12 is probably an example of the last of the Goebel bathing beauty line. Made from pale precolored bisque, she is 6in (15cm) long. Her bathing suit and features were not fired and had worn away in places; for the photograph, she was touched up with a couple of dabs of waterbased acrylic paint, which can be gently washed away with water (a precolored piece should never be scrubbed, for if the painted features are not fired, a vigorous bath will wash them away). She has the lithe adolescent figure and bobbed hair of a flapper, placing her in the 1920s. In 1924, Goebel advertised "Bathing beauties and harem beauties, dancers," so she may date from this period, if not later. She was made in a single mold and lacks the finer details of the other Goebel beauties. Her bathing cap is khaki green and her striped swimsuit is a shade darker. The brown bobbed hair is indicated by two little dabs peeking out from under her cap, and except for her faint one stroke brows and black dot eyes with lid lines, her features had been rubbed away. She is collectible not only because of her size and unusual position, she is also marked in a deeply incised circle on her belly with the crown and intertwined "G" and "W" of Goebel. On the front of her left thigh are the numbers "906" and on her right thigh, the letters "FH". As *Illustration G7* carries the number "901", this may have been a series of model numbers used by the factory on bathing beauties. The letter "H" also appears on both figurines, as well as on *Illustration G4*. The letter "F", followed by another letter, appears on *Illustrations G10 and G11* (as well as on *Illustration H3* in the chapter entitled "One Thousand and One Nights), and may also be an indication of Goebel manufacture.

(Right)
Illustration G9. Postcard dated October 18, 1907.

(Far Right)
Illustration G10. 8in (20cm) tall bisque figurine. Incised "F.N.//760//Dep" over "❀" and stamped "Germany."

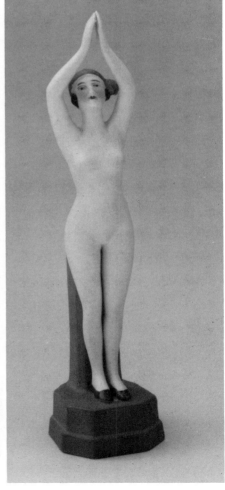

Illustration G11. 8in (20cm) tall bisque figurine. Incised "F.V.//02/1" over "🐝".

Illustration G12. 6in (15cm) long precolored bisque figurine. Incised "906" on left thigh, "FH" on right, and "🐝" on stomach.

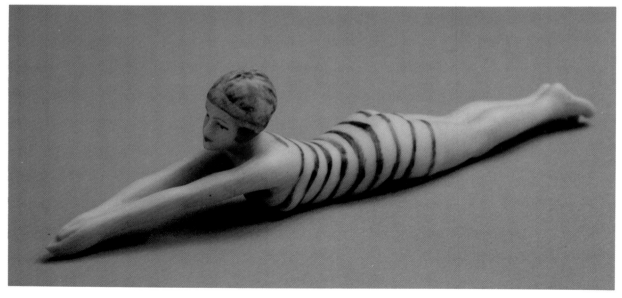

Alfred Pensky

Anyone who has collected bathing beauties and nudies for some time has come across a series of beautifully modeled little flappers, sometimes nude, sometimes in a flocked bathing suit, and occasionally dressed in ribbon. Although hair styles and positions vary, these ladies all share finely detailed, yet realistically proportioned, figures, from the dimpled shoulder blades to the arches of their slender feet. The faces have character and life, often with roguish eyes and mischievous smiles, captured with realism, not exaggeration. Usually, but not always, they sport short wavy hair held in place by a headband. Yet, despite the highest quality of modeling, the bisque is of a precolored slip that varies from too pink to pasty, and the features, usually unfired, are often worn away or muddy colored, as the bisque did not seem to take decoration well. Although rarely marked with a number or country of origin, the family resemblance among these ladies, with their lively expressions and perfectly rendered bodies, is evident.

Although unmarked, a maker can be conjectured. A 1927 advertisement for the company of Alfred Pensky shows a ribbon robed bathing beauty lying on her left side, her right hand clutching a book, as she gives the reader a charming smile. The fine modeling of the body and face is unmistakable, as is her resemblance to many of her sisters. Pensky was a late comer to the world of bathing beauties, first establishing his factory in 1919. Postwar production in Germany, particularly for a small newcomer, presented many problems, from the scarcity of materials and skilled labor to competition with the price cutting Japanese, who had taken advantage of the war to enter the market and had already established a strong presence. In 1925 and 1927, Pensky specifically advertised bathing beauties among his output of all-bisque dolls, baby dolls, pincushions, and candy box decorations. Postwar production and Japanese competition could explain the inferior precolored bisque and the often unfired features that mar these exquisite

Illustration AP1. 2½in (6cm) tall and 3½in (9cm) long precolored bisque figurine. Unmarked. Clothing is not original.

Illustration AP2. 4in (10cm) tall and 4½in (14cm) long china figurine. Incised "7670".

beauties. So unique are the modeling and features of these bathing beauties, conjecturing from the 1927 advertisement, the following ladies can be attributed to Pensky, until a marked figure shows up to negate the hypothesis.

Illustration AP1 is found in a variety of sizes and with various hair styles. 2½in (6cm) tall and 3½in (9cm) long, she displays the same singular qualities of the bather in the advertisement. There is also another link. In 1987, a salesman's sample box of eight bisque figurines of well-modeled women was sold at auction. Among them was a nude whose position and figure was identical to the lady in the 1927 advertisement, although she was lacking a book.

However, another lady in the collection, with molded high heels and painted stockings, held a book while she reclined in a similar pose. All the items appeared to be of precolored bisque and shared the same fine anatomical detailing, and, in the larger items, vivacious expressions. Included among the eight was a seated woman who was a larger version of *Illustration AP1*, although her hair was piled on top of her head and held in place by a bow. Extrapolating from the advertisement to the auction items to *Illustration AP1*, she may well be from the factory of Pensky. Of very pink and somewhat shiny bisque, her modeling is so detailed and realistic, it is as if the artist had shrunk a living woman down to six inches and taken a mold directly off her body. The shoulder blades and spinal channels the hollows at the throat and inside each elbow, the crease in the stomach, the slight protrusion of the pelvic bones, dimples in the knees and small of the back, and the curve of the ankle bones are all indicated with a meticulousness that is extraordinary in such a tiny figurine. The flirty smile that spreads across her heart shaped face creases dimples in her cheeks and narrows her slightly intaglio eyes. Her short curling hair is a pinky caramel, due to the precolored bisque underneath, and is held in place by a reddish hair band. The one stroke brows match her hair and she has blue painted eyes with black pupils and lid lines. The lips, which have been retouched, since the original color had nearly worn away, are full and colored to match her headband (the black lace nightie is also a recent addition). The long slim legs were added at the hip, and while the bisque is sharp and beautifully finished, its too pink coloring is regrettable (I have another version of this figurine, but her precolored complexion is sallow and bleached. While it appears Pensky was able to attract fine sculptors and artisans to his factory, he was unable to acquire the expertise or materials necessary to produce bisque of a consistent quality and attractive color.) She is unmarked. This was a very popular pose and she was copied by the Japanese.

Illustration AP2 is identical to the previously described seated figurine in the salesman's sample, but she has been glazed (Pensky advertised both bisque and china items). 4in (10cm) tall and 4½in (14cm) long, she has the same fantastic modeling as *Illustration AP1*. Instead of a curly bob, her blonde hair is gathered on top of her head by a pink ribbon tied in a large bow on the left side. She has one stroke dark blonde eyebrows, painted blue eyes with black pupils and lid lines, and parted deep red lips. Because of the colored glaze, she has a warm natural flesh tone instead of the often too pink or too pale color that is common among Pensky's bisque pieces. She is lavishly blushed on her cheeks and breasts, with fainter rosy touches on her shoulders and stomach. She is very light for her large size and underneath, where she was not glazed, the exposed grainy bisque has a porous earthenware appearance. She is incised "7670" underneath. I have had a chance to examine the identical figurine, except for a blue hair ribbon, in bisque, and while the bisque was sharp and beautifully finished, the pasty pink precolored complexion detracted from her otherwise lovely features.

3½in (9cm) long, *Illustration AP3* is the china version of *Illustration 5*. Of very pink precolored slip, she has pale blonde hair, one stroke brown brows, black dot eyes with black lid lines, and a deep red mouth. She is unmarked.

Illustration AP4, while only 3in (8cm) long, is beautifully modeled and finished for her size. She was a popular model and I have seen this pose in ladies up to seven inches long. Although this figurine wears a bathing cap and red brown slippers, she also appears in a barefoot version with curly short hair held back by a hair band that still allows a

Illustration AP3. 3½in (9cm) long precolored china figurine. Unmarked.

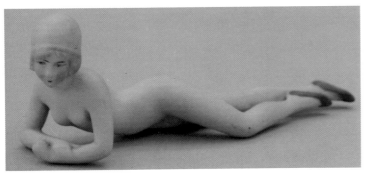

Illustration AP4. 3in (8cm) long precolored bisque figurine. Incised "Germany" on the back of the right thigh and "Germany" and "2829" underneath.

tendril or two to fall towards her shoulders; this is the version that appears in the sample box. Of pale precolored bisque that either did not take or hold color well, she wears a grayish bathing cap almost devoid of color, and has faint dark blonde hair, light black one stroke brows, lid lines, and pupils, and a red dot mouth. The arms were molded in one piece and added at her shoulders. She is incised "Germany" twice, once on the back of her right thigh and again underneath, where she is also incised "2829".

Illustration AP5 is frequently found in a variety of sizes and variations. 4in (10cm) long, she is of pinkish precolored bisque with a slightly oily sheen. She not only has the excellent anatomical modeling that is an element of these attributed Pensky products, but a similar model appeared in the salesman's sample box. Again, linking the 1927 advertisement to the sample box to this figurine links her possibly to Pensky. Her dark blonde curly hair, held by a greenish yellow band, was not fired and the pink bisque is visible where the color has worn away. She has one stroke dark blonde brows, slightly intaglio blue eyes with black lid lines and pupils, and softly smiling full lips (which here have been retouched an orange red). I suspect her right leg was added, as it rests on, but was not molded with, the other leg, but she is so well finished, I cannot be sure of the line of application. She is unmarked. The red negligee and lounge are not original.

Illustration AP5. 4in (10cm) long precolored bisque figurine. Unmarked. Clothing is not original.

Schafer and Vater

Incorporated in 1890 by owners Gustav Schafer and Gunther Vater, Schafer and Vater was a relative late comer among the German bisque manufacturers. However, it quickly became a prolific producer of knick-knacks. While it marketed some rather staid items, such as pin dishes adorned by cute Dutch children, Schafer and Vater is also responsible for some of the most imaginative comical or risqué items produced in bisque. It produced a series of bizarre pitchers, such as a google-eyed man hauling a giant fish on his back, the fish's gaping mouth forming the spout, as well as "nippers," small bottles with comical scenes that were made to contain a "nip" of alcohol. However, the company also seemed to love leggy ladies, and produced a number of beauties.

Illustration SV1 is not one of the Schafer and Vater belles, but it is an example of this factory's sly humor, and often high quality. Here, in a wonderful satire on the sleek swimmers produced by so many of its competitors, a hefty sailor hefts his even heftier honey. The leer on the sailor's finely detailed face certainly suggests he has been at sea a long time and is planning to enjoy his shore leave to the fullest. Beneath his white sailor cap with its black ribbon, his molded thick eyebrows arch over deeply molded side glancing light brown eyes with black lid lines and pupils. His large, somewhat hooked nose, wide smirk, and long light brown whiskers give him the look of a randy Pan. Other than his blue nautical collar and heavy black shoes, there is no other decoration. The face of his companion is not as detailed, as if the artist tired after lavishing so much attention on the sailor. Her pale brown brows are slightly incised and she has only light black lid lines and pupils. Her full cheeks, however, match her seaman sweetheart's and the smile on the parted lips suggests she is not averse to his attentions. She is what one would politely refer to as full-figured, with a light green bathing cap and pale pink suit ruffled at the knees. Behind the amorous couple is a life preserver tied by a tan rope to a greenish stump, open to hold toothpicks or matches. 4in (10cm) tall, the piece is incised

Illustration SV1. 4in (10cm) tall bisque figurine. Incised underneath "7127" and "⚜".

on the base with number "7127" and the Schafer and Vater three point crown over a nine rayed sunburst containing a cursive "R". The bisque is sharp and the modeling excellent, but the decorating, while good, is a tad sloppy. A variation has the sailor dallying with an obese black woman.

Another Schafer and Vater oddity appears in *Illustrations SV2 and SV3*. The 3in (8cm) long, 3¾in (8cm) wide figurine first appears to be a fat, frowning hausfrau asleep in one of two twin beds. The modeling is superb. She wears a molded, deeply ruffled nightcap washed with pale blue and her gray-brown hair is deeply comb-marked. There are fine lines in her forehead and around her eyes. Her one stroke light brown brows are molded, there are black lines between her closed eyelids, and a deeply frowning red mouth. Her sleeveless white nightgown with molded eyelet seems absurdly dainty compared to her broad hunched shoulders and huge breasts. What appear to be her enormous feet stick out from the light blue blanket. The empty bed is concave, as if meant for holding pins, collar studs, or other small items. However, as *Illustration SV3* shows, this unbeautiful dreamer is not sleeping alone. She can be lifted off, and underneath is a stocky little man with a very satisfied smirk. His face has all the fine detail of his companion's. The lank hair and bushy mustache are reddish brown, and the huge feet, which are his, match his equally oversized hands. The piece is incised on the base with the crown and sunburst mark as well as "638", which appears twice.

Schafer and Vater also produced beauties, as well as strange little beasts. *Illustration SV4* is of a 7in (18cm) tall coquette performing a can-can. Her hour glass figure and pronounced cleavage could place her in the gay nineties, perhaps as one of the factory's earliest pieces, but it must be remembered there are often conflicting ideals of feminine form in Western society (for example, contrast the impossibly slim models of *Vogue* with the fleshy femmes in *Playboy*). The figure that was selling dresses at Poiret's fashion house was not necessarily the one packing in patrons at the Folies. I have seen pictures of dancers clad in similar garb from 1908, and her oversized plumed hat certainly evokes the Edwardian, so I would place her definitely within this century. The modeling is superb, and the molding complex. Beneath her huge hat, waves of blonde hair fall to her shoulders. The one stroke brows are dark brown and her eyes, which are gray with black lid lines and pupils, are intaglio with deeply molded upper lids. Her parted light coral lips reveal a row of tiny teeth. The dress and hat are a deep rust brown, but the underskirt, which is held up by her delicate hands, is light green. Her shapely legs are clad in dark brown stockings, which are rather streaked, indicating either a problem with the pigment or merely sloppy application, and she wears orangy heeled pumps. The pebbly base is tan, and forms a hip high vase behind her. The piece was well finished, and the mold lines are hard to distinguish, but it appears that the right arm was added at the elbow and both legs were joined at the skirt. Beneath she is incised with the sunburst and crown mark and "3127".

Illustration SV5 is one of a series of black stockinged ladies. 4in (10cm) tall, she is of a sharp, fine bisque. Her pale blonde hair swirls in deeply combed curls to the shoulder, her one stroke brows are a shade darker blonde. The blue eyes with black pupils and lid lined eyes are beautifully painted, ringed by a deeper flesh tone that gives her a very "bedroom" look. Her nose dots and full mouth are light coral, tiny teeth indicated between her parted lips. Her cheeks are delicately blushed and her very fair complexion is flawless. The white nightgown of slip has a band of pale yellow at the neck, trimmed by twin rows of raised white beads of slip, and it falls in sharply defined folds. Her very shapely legs are clad in black ribbed stockings with red garters, and her tan pumps with gold buckles resemble the footwear of *SV4*. The arms were added at the straps of her nightgown, cleverly hiding the addition line. The little finger on her right hand has been repaired, and should have been daintily raised. Despite this damage, she is still a collectible and desirable figurine. She is incised underneath with the figures "2862" and "70", and a freehand "6" marked in black.

She does not carry the Schafer and Vater mark, but the same figurine in another collection is incised on the base with the sunburst mark. Why would the same figurines be marked in one case, and not the other? Usually, the mark and numerals were part of the mold, so each piece carries the mark. However, in the case of many of the Schafer and Vater figurines I have examined, the marks do not have the softened edges of mold incised mark, but have sharp deep edges, as if they were stamped in during the greenware stage. The marks may be in different places on the same model of figurine, and, as in the case of *Illustration SV2*, the mark may appear twice on the same piece, as if it was decided the first mark was not clear enough, so it was repeated. Sometimes, while the edges of the mark are sharp, the mark is faint and shallow, as if it were not stamped hard enough or the figurine had been allowed to dry too long. If Schafer and Vater chose to stamp its marks instead of incising them in the mold, this would have given the factory the option of deleting its mark from flawed or imperfect pieces, which it could sell as "seconds" at a cheaper rate, or of selling unmarked pieces to a distributor who wished to sell the pieces under its name.

Illustration SV6 is from the same series. Her hair is also pale blonde and she has the same deeply modeled curls, excellent bisque, and fair complexion. 5in (13cm) long, she has one stroke blonde brows, and while her painted blue eyes with black lid lines and pupils do not have the vampish shadowing, there are red lid lines. Her nose dots and lids are faint coral, with a darker line under the upper lip. The white nightgown has short sleeves trimmed in light yellow, but no beaded decoration. The gown rides up the thighs to expose her white knickers, and her leg and footwear are identical to *Illustration SV5's*, but the shoes lack the gold buckles. Her rather uninterested looking cat is black and white, with a light coral mouth. The figurine is incised underneath with

"2863/1" (in this case, the number appears to have been incised in the mold) and a painted freehand "III" in black.

Illustration SV7 is incised "2865", which appears to have been stamped. 4in (10cm) high, her decoration and quality are so identical with *Illustration SV5's*, they must certainly have been produced during the same period. While she does have the same sultry eye makeup as *Illustration SV5*, her downcast, half closed eyes have only curved black lid lines and pupils. Otherwise she has the same decoration from the curling pale blonde hair to the gold buckled tan slipper. She is pulling her nightgown completely free of her right breast, which required the yoke of her gown to be molded separately and added at the greenware stage, as were both her arms. I have seen other figurines of this model, but the decoration and finishing were poor. As each piece was assembled, decorated, and finished by hand, the skill of any individual in the manufacturing process could significantly alter the quality of each piece.

Since *Illustrations SV5 through SV7* are all clearly from the same series, there must be a "2864" lolling about in her chemise or kicking up her black stockinged legs. Could there also be a "2861" or a "2866"? Schafer and Vater certainly seemed to have loved long legged ladies and there may well be more. *Illustrations SV8 and SV9*, while not marked with any "2860" number, and, though charming, are not of the quality of the previous three, do appear to be relations. 3¼in (8cm) high, *Illustration SV8's* hair is more orangy than *Illustrations' SV5 through SV7*, and although deeply comb-marked, does not have the free flowing curls. She has a higher color, with one stroke dark blonde brows, blue eyes with black pupils and black and red lid lines, and parted reddish lips. Her white gown does have the yellow trim and raised dots at the neckline and the folds and creases are sharply molded. She wears black ribbed stockings and orange-tan pumps that lack gold buckles. Although she is marked only "3" underneath, an example in my collection is incised "68." If she is indeed part of the "2860" series, this would imply there is a "2866" and a "2867." This figurine has been seen in a black version as well.

Compared to the others, *Illustration SV9* seems rather chunky, her arms and hands appearing especially thick and heavy. But she is still appealing and collectible. Her color and decoration are similar to *SV8's*. Just over 5¼in (14cm) long, she is incised with a freehand "34" underneath.

Illustration SV10 is not marked, but she shares so many characteristics of known Schafer and Vater women, the detailed pale blonde hair, flirtatious glance, parted lips, beaded trim, and, of course, the shapely legs clad in dark stockings, she can be attributed to this maker until a marked piece comes along. 6¼in (16cm) tall, her wavy light blonde hair is twisted up into a topknot. Her dark blonde brows arch over side glancing intaglio blue eyes with black pupils and lid lines, as well as dark pink lid lines both above and below her eyes. She has coral nose dots and parted lips. Although her long arms are slim, her body is rather voluptuous as is well revealed by her outfit. Instead of a dress, she appears to be wearing only a long piece of molded pale yellow cloth

that is "fastened" under her left arm and at her left hip (with a gap in between that exposes the pale flesh underneath). Pink straps around her neck barely pull the makeshift outfit over her full breasts. The whole is decorated lavishly with beaded white trim at the yoke and white and gold beaded florets throughout. Similar flowing, and scanty, outfits clad many an Art Nouveau nymph, but no muse of Alfonse Mucha ever wore black ribbed stockings and orange-tan pumps with gold buckles. In her right hand she offers a pale blue wine glass, perhaps filled from the green urn trimmed with white grape leaves attached to her at the rear left. The arms, the urn, the entire right flap of her robe, and even her left leg outstretched to its stocking top, all appear to have been added. Her complexion is pale and flawless, the bisque sharp and beautifully modeled, and the decoration excellent. Although any maker could be proud of this piece, she is marked only with an incised "4411", which appears to have been stamped underneath.

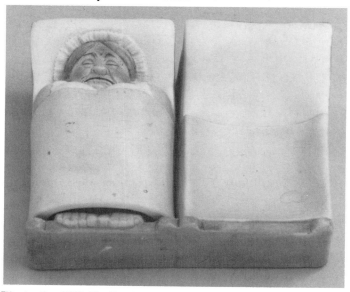

Illustration SV2. 3in (8cm) long and 3¾in (8cm) wide bisque figurine. Incised underneath twice "638" and "✿".

Illustration SV3. *Illustration SV2* with upper portion removed.

Illustration SV4. 7in (18cm) tall bisque figurine attached to vase. Incised underneath "3127" and 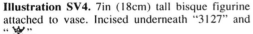.

Illustration SV5. 4in (10cm) tall bisque figurine. Marked underneath with a freehand "6" in black and incised "2862" and "70".

Illustration SV6. 5in (13cm) long bisque figurine. Marked underneath with a freehand "III" in black and an incised "2863/1".

80

Illustration SV8. 3¼in (8cm) tall bisque figurine. Marked "3". *Private Collection.*

Illustration SV7. 4in (10cm) tall bisque figurine. Incised underneath "2865".

Illustration SV9. 5¼in (14cm) long bisque figurine. Incised underneath "34". *Private Collection.*

Illustration SV10. 6¼in (16cm) tall bisque figurine. Incised underneath "4411".

Little Squirts

These hollow naughties were meant to be filled with liquid (most likely water) and when a rubber bulb perched atop the figurine was squeezed, the liquid would squirt from an appropriate orifice. Although they take many forms, "squirters" (as I have christened them) share a number of characteristics. They are small, generally not more than 3½in (9cm) high, have a small lipped opening at the top, and one or two tiny holes for the water to squirt out of. All once had a rubber bulb (resembling that of an old-fashioned eyedropper), but it is almost always missing, although sometimes traces of the rubber may remain. If a collector is fortunate enough to find a squirter with the original bulb attached, the rubber is usually hardened and frail. However, any squirter can be made to perform by filling it with water and blowing into its top opening.

Numerous times I have had antique dealers describe squirters as perfume bottles. Although they could be used

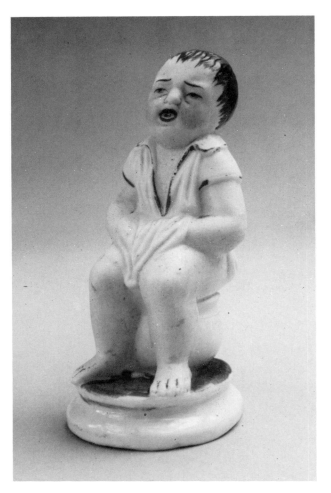

Illustration S1. 4½in (12cm) tall bisque potty baby. Marked underneath with a freehand "2".

for perfume, I doubt that was their intended purpose. The majority are made of porous bisque and are not glazed inside, which would contribute to the contamination or evaporation of the perfume. There were no metal fittings, the rubber bulb slipping over the lip of the opening on the figurine, so not only was the squirter not airtight, but the perfume could come in direct contact with the rubber bulb, which would adversely affect both. The exit hole is often in the middle portion of the figurine, so any perfume below that level would be wasted. Further, the liquid comes out in a thin stream, not a misting spray, and can cover a surprising distance, a costly way to apply perfume. Another story I have heard is that they were made for brothels, who gave them away as souvenirs to clientele. I suppose it is possible that a house of ill repute could have ordered a box or two for this purpose, but again, I do not believe this was the intended destination of squirters. It is doubtful that any regular customer of a bordello would want a tangible advertisement of his patronage. One would also question whether there were enough brothels or patrons to account for the sizable number of squirters produced. Squirters were openly advertised in the catalogues of such prestigious doll making firms as J.D. Kestner, so their manufacture was not hidden or kept secret, which one would suspect would be the case if they were only meant as mementos for the oldest profession. The most common figurines are of little boys, not women, and they closely resemble the "potty" and piano babies that were so popular as decorative knick-knacks around the turn of the century. All this suggests squirters were marketed as nothing more than cute, silly novelties.

Illustration S1 is a typical bisque potty baby, clearly the first cousin of the squirter. 4½in (12cm) tall, he appears to be in dire throes as he sits on his chamberpot. His medium brown hair is brushstroked around his face, his frowning brows are single strokes of dark brown. The painted blue eyes have black pupils and lid lines, and his tongue is visible in his open mouth. The white nightshirt, here trimmed in blue, is the typical dress for potty and piano babies, as well as the squirters. His molded base is glazed and trimmed in gold. He is marked only with a freehand "2" underneath. The bisque is sharp and the modeling and decoration are well done for this type of figurine. Such potty babies can be found in all sizes, sexes, races, and situations. They were sometimes made in pairs, one in distress similar to that in the illustration and the other grinning contentedly (some people refer to them as "Johnny Can't" and "Johnny Can"), or there may be two struggling for space on the same tiny chamberpot (often one is a boy or Caucasian, while the other is female or Black). They are not at all uncommon, and their number and variety implies they were once popular household decorations.

Illustration S2 is a squirter, and shows the close relationship between the potty babies and squirters. Just 3 1/4in (8cm) tall, this little girl also seems to be in distress. Her peaked bonnet is trimmed in orange and ties with a large bow of the same color. Bangs of light brown peak out from under her bonnet and she has the same one stroke frowning brows as *Illustration S1*. Her eyes are only black lid lines with pupils, and her open, grimacing lips are the same orange as found in her bonnet and on the cuffs of her short nightshirt. Between her pudgy legs straddling the chamberpot is a small hole for the water to squirt out from. The bisque is fairly sharp, and the folds in her nightshirt and bow are nicely modeled. Like most of these figurines, the decoration was done in haste and kept to a minimum (white nightshirts and chamberpots saved a lot of time, since only the face and limbs had to be tinted and decorated), but is adequate for this type of figurine. She is incised "1645" on the back.

Illustration S3 is another squirter variation of the potty baby. 3½in (9cm) tall, this little boy seems a bit more content than the previous illustrations. Traces of the lost rubber bulb can be seen around the lip of the opening atop his head. He is wearing a nightcap with a tassel hanging down the back, light brown hair framing his face. His single stroke brows are the same light brown, the painted eyes are only black lid lines and pupils, and his slightly parted lips are the same brick red as the two molded pom-poms hanging down the front of his nightshirt. He is incised "13570" on the back.

Plump little boys answering the call of nature are the most popular form of squirter, and *Illustrations S4 and S5* are variations of the most common type. The "Universal-Spielwarenkatalog 1928" displayed such a squirter among its all-bisque dolls and novelties and J.D. Kestner included a similar squirter in its 1930 catalogue. *Illustration S4* is 3½in (9cm) tall and is the finer of the two. A blue knit stocking cap sits upon his masses of deeply comb-marked blonde curls, and all his modeling is deep and sharp. His one stroke brows are blond and the slightly intaglio eyes have black lid lines and pupils. The lips are deep red and he has a double chin and creases of fat in his neck. He is a most well fed lad, with creases and rolls of fat all over. His white nightshirt is trimmed with blue at the neck and his right hand delicately holds his intimate part, from which would issue the stream of water. The even complexion coat is rosy and he is of excellent bisque. He is incised "1423." on the back and has the remains of "Germany" stamped in red. Since after March 1, 1891, all imports coming to this country were supposed to be marked with the country of origin, some dealers insist these little figurines must predate that law since so few are marked with anything besides number. However, doll and wholesale catalogues featured them as late as 1930, so they were produced and imported well after the 1891 date. The faint stamp on this example suggests that many of these little figurines may have been marked, but that the stamp wore away with time and handling. Also, many were probably marked on the cardboard boxes they were shipped in, instead of on the figurine itself.

Illustration S5 is 3¾in (10cm) tall. He is not simply another issue of *Illustration S4* from a larger mold, for even though his pose is similar, there are many small differences between the two. His face is rounder and flatter with deep dimples in the cheeks, his legs are farther apart, and the positions of the hands are slightly different. The modeling is not as sharp and the decoration is rather sloppy, the pale complexion coat smearing over onto the white nightshirt, one eye having a heavier lid line than the other, and the lips crookedly painted. His hair, one stroke brows, and lid lines are light brown, the eyes black dots. There are no marks. This was a popular pose and appears in many different variations, so *Illustrations S4 and S5* are probably from different factories despite their similarities.

Another frequently found squirter was copied after the famous, and aptly named, Manneken Pis statue of Brussels. The bronze statue was designed by Jerome Duquesnoy in 1619 (the current statue is a replacement; the original was stolen by soldiers in the eighteenth century) and is a popular landmark and tourist attraction. *Illustration S6* was clearly inspired by Manneken Pis. 3½in (9cm) high, he is of excellent bisque and is nicely decorated. His deeply comb-marked blonde hair is topped by a green lip for the rubber bulb. The one stroke brows are deep blond. His downcast eyes have heavy lids with black lid lines and pupils, and there are coral nose dots that match the tiny mouth. The modeling is of highest quality and includes nipples, dimples on his back, and fat creases behind his knees. The complexion coat is pale and even. He stands on a three tier gray platform. which is incised "4313" on the back.

While the previous little boys went sedately about their business, *Illustration S7* seems genuinely surprised with his ability. 3½in (9cm) tall, he is one of the many character and comic bisque figurines that were produced by such factories as Schafer and Vater following the turn of the century. His blue knit cap fails to cover his protruding ears, and his orangy dabbed brows seem to arch with astonishment. The somewhat bulging eyes have gray lid lines and large black pupils, his nose is snub to the extreme, and his thin deep red lips stretch into a half-smile. Fat, oversized hands hold up his white nightshirt, and his knuckles, navel, and baggy bowlegs are blushed. The large pigeon-toed feet allow him to stand sturdily by himself. He is incised on the back "Germany" over "5607". For this type of novelty, the decoration and modeling are of high quality.

The seated boy in *Illustration S8* wears an unusual pink hat with an incised sunburst design. 2½in (6cm) tall, his fine bisque, decoration, and pale complexion suggest he may be an earlier example. His blond curls are deeply comb-marked, and his one stroke brows are a shade darker. The eyes have molded lids and laugh lines in the corners, but only painted pupils. His puckered light coral lips were painted in two parts. The pale blue trim on the white nightshirt matches the deeply textured socks. The nightshirt itself has a suggestion of gathers at the neck and, where the hem is turned up, ribbing in the cloth. The complexion coat is very pale and even. Cradling his privates with both hands,

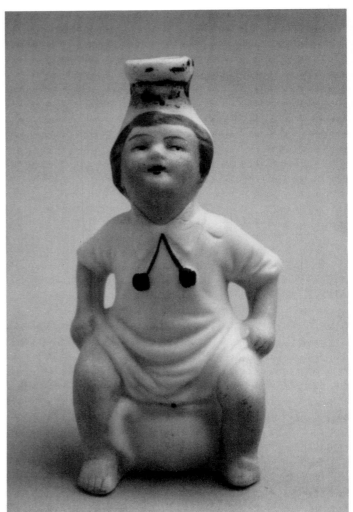

Illustration S2. 3¼in (8cm) tall bisque squirter. Incised "1645" on back.

Illustration S3. 3½in (9cm) tall bisque squirter. Incised "13570" on back.

he can send an arc of water upwards when squirted. He is incised "4309" underneath. Because his quality compares with that of *Illustration S6* and because they both are marked with a four digit number beginning with "43", one is tempted to venture a guess that they may be from the same factory.

Like the potty and piano babies, the little boy squirters also came in Black. There was a market for humorous figurines with ethnic stereotypes and Blacks often appeared. Some such figurines were rather gentle in their jibes, but others, then considered cute and comical, now would be regarded as tasteless and racist. *Illustrations S9 and S10* are more unusual Black versions of the little boy squirters, and avoid the more vicious stereotyping seen in some comic bisques of the period. *Illustration S9* may well be from the same manufacturer as *Illustration S7*, for not only does he share the same (although thinner) bowlegs and joined feet as *Illustration S7*, he is incised on the back "5605" and "Germany" in the same type of lettering. Instead of the expected nightcap, his opening lip is disguised as a hat of green leaves sitting on his kinky black hair. His features are Negroid, but other than his very large eyes, are not exaggerated. The

mouth is indicated by a red dab between his wide lips. His complexion is very deep brown and glossy and, as is common with many black dolls and figurines, the skin tone is not even (darker colors are difficult to apply evenly on bisque and may require several firings. This may be one reason why blue-eyed blondes dominated the bisque world). He wears only a short white nightshirt. The bisque is sharp and the modeling good. This squirter is 3in (8cm) tall.

Unmarked and of lesser quality, *Illustration S10* is still very desirable because of his race. 3½in (9cm) tall, he retains what may be his original rubber bulb, now ossified beyond use. Although his skin is very black, his features are not, and he has been seen in a Caucasian version. The eyes have only a thin rim of white and his mouth is indicated only by a reddish smear. He wears a white cap and rompers, trimmed in bright pink. The rompers have molded buttons, the last of which is undone so he may "relieve" himself. He is quite sturdy and can stand alone.

Adult squirters are far rarer and seem to belong almost entirely to the female gender. Unlike the little boys, the lady squirters probably appealed only to men (adult male squirters may have been too sexually suggestive for marketing, and

(Right)
Illustration S4. 3½in (9cm) tall bisque squirter. Incised "1423" on back and faintly stamped in red "Germany."

(Far Right)
Illustration S5. 3¾in (10cm) tall bisque squirter. Unmarked.

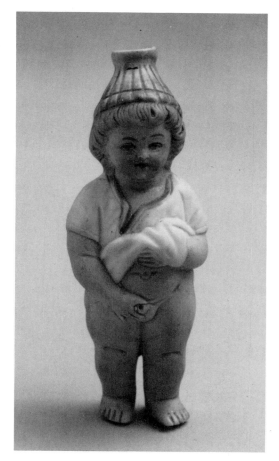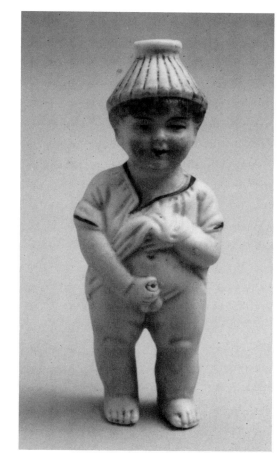

(Right)
Illustration S6. 3½in (9cm) tall bisque squirter modeled after the Manneken Pis statue in Brussels. Incised "4313" on back.

(Far Right)
Illustration S7. 3½in (9cm) tall bisque squirter. Incised "Germany//5607" on back.

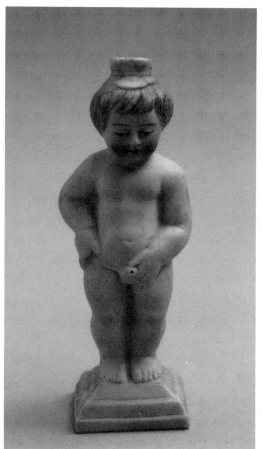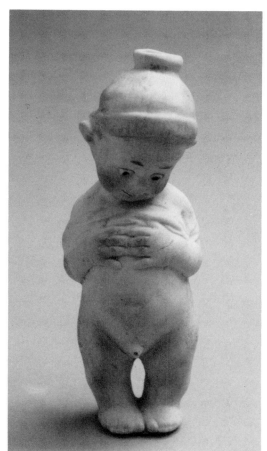

Illustration S8. 2½in (6cm) tall bisque squirter. Incised "4309" underneath.

it is unlikely many women would have purchased them). The ladies fall into three categories: (1) squirt through one or both breasts; (2) double entendre in which the water spurts out of the mouth of a cat perched on a woman's lap; and, (3) the rarest group, female figurines with the hole between their legs.

3¾in (10cm) tall, and of exceptional bisque, *Illustration S11* squirts water from her left breast. Her blonde wavy hair is tied up with a pink ribbon, which disguises the opening lip. Her one stroke brows are dark blonde, the blue painted eyes have black lid lines and pupils, and her parted lips are slightly smiling. The complexion is flawless and peachy, her pink chemise with molded eyelet trim falling off her shoulders. Although her right hand appears to be trying to hold up her chemise, the other cups her bare left breast. Except for her concave back, the lovely coloring continues around the back. She is faintly stamped "Germany" underneath.

Illustration S12 is another excellent quality squirter. 3½in (9cm) tall, her light brown wavy hair swirls up into a topknot that disguises the upper opening. The one stroke brows are dark brown and the blue painted eyes have black lid lines and pupils. The gently smiling lips are slightly parted and she has dimples in her cheeks. Her head and shoulders rise out of a swirl of green petals sitting atop a white pedestal trimmed in rose. Both her bare breasts squirt water. She is unmarked.

Although *Illustrations S13 and S14* are similar poses, they are not from the same mold, and possibly not from the same manufacturer. *Illustration S13* has beautiful flowing ash blonde hair with windblown curls, the topknot hiding the upper opening. The one stroke brows are dark brown and the eyes have molded upper and lower lids with black lid lines and intaglio pupils. She is slightly smiling and has dimples in her cheeks. Her chemise is very pale yellow and has molded eyelet trim. Each hand cups a bare breast and she has an opening in both breasts. She is incised "1486" across the back and is 3in (8cm) tall. Perhaps she is the big sister of *Illustration S4*, who is incised "1423." This squirter was crudely copied by the Japanese in coarse white bisque with poor decoration.

Illustration S14 is broader and her head is larger. Her wavy blonde hair is neatly parted in the center and her whole aspect is more demure. The one stroke brows are dark blonde and the blue painted eyes have red and black lid lines. The lips are slightly parted and there are faint dimples. Her chemise is uncolored and the eyelet trim is different from *Illustration S13*. She is more buxom than *Illustration S13* and her paler bisque is slightly oily; at 2¾in (9cm) tall, she is also slightly shorter. There are no marks.

Another series of squirters involves women and cats. "Puss" has long been an affectionate name for a young girl or woman and "pussy" is a vulgar slang term for female privates. The next three squirters use the cat as a double entendre. *Illustration S15* is 3½in (9cm) high and is of a little girl dressed in Kate Greenaway style. Her floppy green mobcap forms the lip for the absent rubber bulb and her deeply comb-marked light brown hair falls in long curls over her shoulders and down her back. Her face is delicately painted with fine one stroke brown brows, black lid lines and pupils, and a deep coral mouth. The pale green dress has white ruffles at the cuffs and neckline. She has gathered the full skirt in the front, exposing her bare knees, the ruffled edge of her knickers, white stockings, and black slippers. Out of the folds of the skirt, just below her waist, peeks the head of a black kitten who "spits" the water. She is beautifully molded and well decorated for her size, but is incised only "1656." on the back. As *Illustration S2* is incised "1645", they may be from the same series and factory.

Although incised "4312" on the base and of a less sharp bisque, *Illustration S16* bears a certain family resemblance to *Illustration S15*. 2½in (6cm) tall, she lacks the innocence of the previous example. Definitely a woman, as attested by the cleavage exposed by her low cut dress, she still wears a Kate Greenaway type pink bonnet with molded eyelet beneath the brim, her blonde hair falling in curls about her shoulders. The back of the bonnet forms the opening lip, and yellowish traces of hardened rubber still adhere to it. Her face is as carefully decorated as *Illustrations S15's*, although she has been given very beestung lips, as if she is puckering. The dress is a shade deeper green than that in *Illustration S15*, with a low white bodice. As she squats, a black kitten peers from the folds between her spread knees, its mouth the exit for the water. The ruffles of her petticoats are indicted and she wears white stockings and pink slippers.

2¾in (7cm) tall, *Illustration S17* has no bonnet to disguise the opening lip. Her dark blonde hair is swept on top of her head with carefully combed curls lying on her shoulders and neck. The facial features are well painted, with one stroke dark blonde brows, black lid lines and pupils, and deep coral mouth. The low square neckline, which reveals ample cleavage, is trimmed in white edging, as are the cuffs of her short sleeves. The dress is light blue and she wears deep pink stockings with black slippers. The cat peeking between her legs has gray ears, black pupils, and a mouth outlined in red. Like the others, it "spits" water. She is incised "12054".

The hardest to find squirters are women who squirt directly from between their legs, perhaps because of the sexual overtones. *Illustration S18* is also unusual because of her long black stockings, a favorite accessory of risqué "French" postcards (and a much sought after detail by collectors). 3in (8cm) tall, she has shoulder length orange-blonde curling hair, her topknot forming the opening lip. The single stroke brows and lid lines are dark blonde, and the eyes are blue-black dots. The heart shaped mouth is deep red. The neckline of her white slip, which has slipped below her breasts, is trimmed with molded eyelet. One hand flips up the slip edge between her spread legs, revealing the hole from where the water would squirt. The black stockings are glossy and the slippers pink. Her chamberpot was actually molded separately and joined to her in the greenware stage. One wonders why the unknown manufacturer went through so much trouble, when it could have easily been made in a single mold. Perhaps this allowed the maker to use the separately molded chamberpot for other items. She is incised "4321" on the back of the chamberpot, which indicates she may be from the same factory and series as *Illustration S16*, and therefore possibly a big sister to the little boys in *Illustrations S6 and S8*, whose four digit numbers also begin with "43"; all of these "43" figurines are of high quality bisque, modeling, and decoration for this type of novelty.

4in (10cm) long, *Illustration S19* reclines on her left side. Her light brown hair is twisted into a high topknot, which is the lip opening. The one stroke brows are dark brown, as are her lid lines. Her eyes are deep blue dots and the mouth deep coral. The white slip, which is sliding from her shoulders, has ruffles around the low neckline. She coyly tugs up the hem of the slip, exposing the hole between her legs. Her thigh high black stockings are ribbed and she has white slippers. There are no marks.

Illustration S20, which is 4¼in (11cm) long, is a variation of *Illustration S19*, and is either from another company or a later issue. She lacks the sharp details of *Illustration S19*, and the decoration is cruder. The dark blonde hair is less elaborate, and the eyebrows and lid lines are an odd red-brown. The eyes are dots of deep blue and the mouth a tiny dab of red. The neckline of her slip is trimmed with molded eyelet and her ribbed stockings are light blue. She is incised "512" over "Germany" on the back.

Illustration S21, to some minds, crosses the line from risqué to vulgar, and is the only female squirter in this group to actually depict genitalia. 3¾in (8cm) tall, she is of good bisque, but rather mediocre modeling. The ash blonde hair forms a topknot for the now missing rubber bulb, although traces of it are still present. Her flat, expressionless face is well painted, with blonde one stroke brows, black lid lines and pupils, and orange-red mouth. The sleeveless white shirt is trimmed in blue at the neckline and the knickers are a shade lighter. A black line between her legs marks her intimate parts, from where the stream of water would issue. Although the modeling is not as sharp or detailed as the previous figurines, she is ingeniously balanced, the trailing end of her shift forming a third "leg," so she can stand alone. She is incised "1505" on the back.

(Above Left)
Illustration S9. 3in (8cm) tall bisque squirter. Incised "Germany//5605" on back.

(Above Right)
Illustration S10. 3½in (9cm) tall bisque squirter, which retains what may be its original rubber bulb. Unmarked.

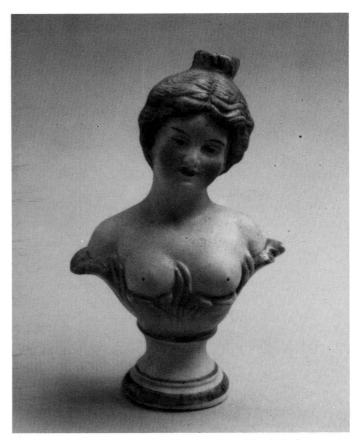

Illustration S11. 3¾in (10cm) tall bisque squirter. Stamped faintly with "Germany" underneath.

Illustration S12. 3½in (9cm) tall bisque squirter. Unmarked.

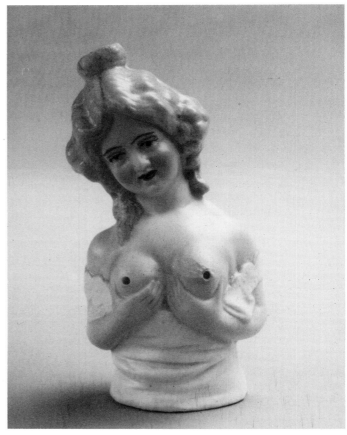

Illustration S13. 3in (8cm) tall bisque squirter. Incised "1486" on back.

Illustration S14. 2¾in (9cm) tall bisque squirter. Unmarked.

Illustration S16. 2½in (6cm) tall bisque squirter. Incised "4312" on back.

Illustration S15. 3½in (9cm) tall bisque squirter. Incised "1656" on back.

Illustration S17. 2¾in (7cm) tall bisque squirter. Incised "12054" on back.

Illustration S19. 4in (10cm) long bisque squirter. Unmarked.

Illustration S18. 3in (8cm) tall bisque squirter. Incised "4321" on back of chamberpot.

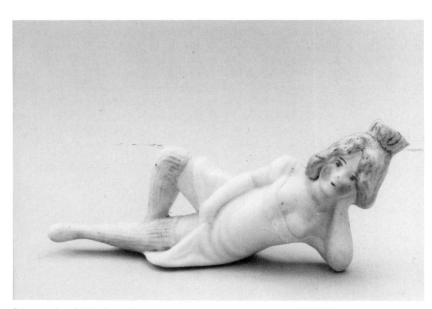

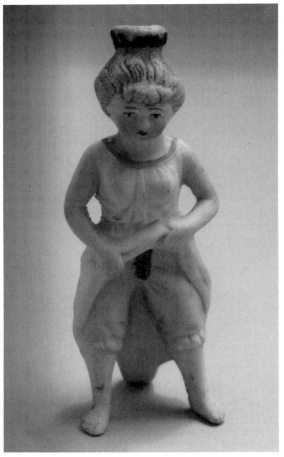

Illustration S20. 4¼in (11cm) long bisque squirter. Incised "512//Germany" on back.

Illustration S21. 3¾in (8cm) tall bisque squirter. Incised "1505" on back.

The Flip Side

Sitting on a shelf among the other knick-knacks and collectibles is a bisque figurine of a seated woman in an old fashioned dress, her full skirt spread demurely around her. The unwary antiquer, won over by her charm, picks her up, turning her over in search of a mark. The surprised shopper discovers the lady of his attentions has neglected to fasten her split knickers and her nude nether region is exposed to view. Instead of a simple figurine, the prize is a flip-over naughty.

Although flip-over naughties, dubbed by the author as "flippers," were probably produced by the thousands in German factories, they are not too common today. Despite their often excellent quality, they were considered inexpensive novelties, and families discarded them instead of passing them on with the more proper heirlooms (no doubt the desire to preserve the memory of the deceased in the most favorable light also played a part. A doting grandmother can proudly hand her grandson his grandfather's prized pocketwatch. Handing him his grandfather's bare bottomed belle is another matter). Also, unlike most figurines, they were meant to be handled, but, being made of bisque and china, were not really made for such treatment, and many were broken over the years.

Illustration FP1 is a typical flipper. Just 4in (10cm) tall, she is of fine, sharp bisque. Her Kate Greenaway style dress is pale green, decorated with raised gilt dots, and her beribboned blue bonnet, trimmed with a single pink rose, does not restrain her flowing dark blonde curls. The one stroke brows are dark brown and she has painted blue eyes with black pupils between deeply molded lids and slightly smiling beestung coral lips. Her face and hands are delicately tinted, but her legs, ending in gold slippers, were left white to represent stockings. When she is turned over, as seen in *Illustration FP2*, she presents her bare buttocks, framed by the ruffles of her white petticoats and pantaloons. Like most of these figurines she carries no mark. Her size and design would have made her difficult to mark, and since she was nothing more than an inexpensive novelty, her manufacturer had no incentive to really try.

Illustration FP3 harks back to a time when a manufacturer could be both racist and sexist with impunity. 2½in (6cm) tall and 5in (13cm) wide, she almost appears to be reclining. The deeply incised and well modeled features are only lightly decorated, with intaglio brown eyes and dark coral parted lips that reveal molded teeth. Although her complexion is faintly golden and her black hair is caught up in Oriental fashion with golden tipped hairpins, she is no more Japanese than the three little maids of "The Mikado." She looks rather like a Gibson girl preparing for a costume party. It is a colorful costume, consisting of a bright green kimono trimmed in pink with a yellow and red striped obi. The blue flower at her waist matches the parasol she holds in her right hand. Incised at the hem of the kimono, just above her incongruous black stockings and tan slippers, is the incised caption, "The Yellow Peril." As seen in *Illustration FP4*, when flipped over, her nude behind is exposed, along with her very un-Japanese knickers, ruffled petticoats, and black stockings. Although she is unmarked, her features and dress, as well as fine quality, resemble those of the more discrete Japanese ladies who decorate vases made by the German firm of Schafer and Vater, also known for its comical, and often ribald, figurines.

The 6in (15cm) long lady in *Illustration FP5* also carries an umbrella, as well as a white cat sporting a pink bow. Her wide brimmed bonnet is bright green, as are her umbrella and the laces of her bodice, while her dress is pale blue. Tendrils of dark blonde hair peek out from under her bonnet and she has matching one stroke brows, slightly intaglio blue eyes with black lid lines and pupils, and full deep coral lips. Although her face and shoulders are rosy, her arms have been left white to indicate long gloves and her legs treated the same for stockings. The pink bow at her waist matches that of her cat, and she wears tan slippers. These tan slippers, and her blushing bottom, are the only items that have been decorated on the reverse, seen in *Illustration FP6*. The bisque is sharp and smooth and the decoration excellent.

Illustration FP7 also cradles a cat. 3in (8cm) tall, she is very finely modeled for this type of figurine. Her graceful arms are separate from her body and skirt, requiring the upper torso be molded separately and applied at the waist to avoid undercutting. Her face is framed by windblown dark blonde hair and she has matching one stroke brows, slightly intaglio pale blue eyes with black lid lines and pupils between deeply molded lids, and gently smiling coral lips. The pale blue gown is decorated with florettes of raised gold dots, and has gold straps and neckline. Her cat is gray and white, his molded collar left untinted. She wears black stockings and slightly heeled red-brown shoes with gilt buckles. *Illustration FP8* shows the flip side, and she is fully decorated underneath, including a bright yellow underslip.

Illustration FP9 is of yet another femme and her feline. 5½in (14cm) wide and 3in (8cm) high, this china piece was copied extensively, and poorly, by the Japanese. Her light brown hair falls in ringlets to her bare shoulders, the one stroke brows are dark brown, and the downglancing blue eyes have black lid lines and pupils. Her orange-red mouth gasps with surprise and her cheeks, throat, and nipples are generously blushed. The white nightdress has slid completely off her shoulders and breasts, the full skirt swirling

Illustration FP1. 4in (10cm) tall bisque flipper. Unmarked.

Illustration FP2. Underside of *Illustration FP1*.

Illustration FP3. 2½in (6cm) tall bisque flipper. Caption reads "The Yellow Peril." Unmarked.

Illustration FP4. Underside of *Illustration FP3*.

Illustration FP5. 6in (15cm) long bisque flipper. Unmarked.

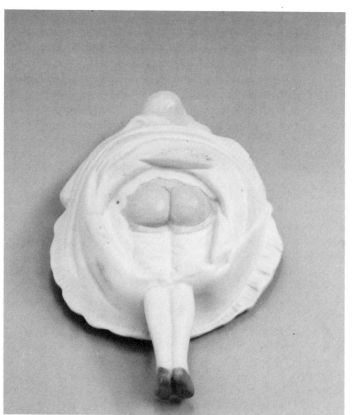

Illustration FP6. Underside of *Illustration FP5.*

to form a small dish. Her right leg, with its pale green stocking and slightly darker pump, is exposed to the knee, and her left foot is visible beneath her gown's hem. On the edge of the dish, a plump gray and white cat seems to be trying to peer underneath her mistress. A clue to the object of the cat's curiosity is the phrase, "Where is the mouse?", in gilt block letters across the indentation of the dish. *Illustration FP10* exposes the mouse, the lady's bottom, and the cause of her distress. Marked underneath with "Made in Germany" in small gilt letters, she is finely modeled and decorated.

Illustration FP11 is a variation of the theme. Instead of a three dimensional figurine, this 4¾in (12cm) long china dish has a bas-relief of a nymph reclining against deep green-gold trimmed flowers and grass. Her long flowing hair is blonde, the one stroke brows light brown, her eyes black dots with matching lid lines, the lips orange, and her drapery a slightly iridescent pink. Curiously, the top edge of the dish is flat, so it can stand, but the nymph would be upside down. The reverse, as seen in *Illustration FP12,* reveals a standing woman, her back to a window, nightdress parted to expose her buttocks (which are the only tinted item) and a chamberpot. The finishing and decoration are sloppy, with large undecorated areas left around the nymph figure. This flipper is incised "46" near the top of the back side.

Illustration FP13 is an extremely elaborate flipper. On the front side, within a deep pink rococo frame, a naked cupid with yellow wings clutches his bow and arrow as he peeks through a "brocade" pale blue curtain with yellow fringe. In the upper left hand corner, in freehand deep green letters, is the caption, "Oh! You pretty Gibson girl!" However, anyone who, spurred by the cupid's enthusiasm, turns over the flipper is likely to be disappointed. Instead of an elegant, slender woman of the type immortalized by artist Charles Dana Gibson, the reverse, shown in *Illustration FP14,* carries an obese female in her white chemise, one fat leg clad in a ribbed black stocking as she stands over a chamberpot. Her braided dark blonde hair is tied with a light green ribbon and her one stroke brows match her hair. The light brown painted eyes have black and red lid lines and her parted lips are pale coral. 5½in (17cm) tall, the details are all sharply molded and the bisque and finishing are excellent.

Also 5½in (17cm) tall, the flipper in *Illustration FP15* has what appears to be two plump cherries lying on a bed of light and dark green finely detailed leaves. The back, revealed in *Illustration FP16,* shows instead the ripe cherries are actually the derrieres of two bathing beauties wearing pale pink swimsuits and lace up bathing slippers. Their tousled blonde hair is especially well done and they have dark blonde one stroke brows, red and black lid lines, blue painted eyes with black pupils, and parted coral lips. The good quality bisque is sharp and the modeling and decoration well done for this type of novelty.

Illustration FP17 is an unusual flipper because of what it does not reveal. 5½in (17cm) wide, the top portion is of two women who have just dived into a swirling blue pond, with only their heads and bare shoulders appearing above the water. Behind them, on a dark brown clothesline strung between tan posts, are two pairs of white bloomers billowing in the breeze. However, the collector who, with a knowing wink, turns over the flipper is not treated to beauty bare, but instead, as shown in *Illustration FP18*, to the ladies' lower torsos discreetly clad in pink panties. The women are blonde, one wearing a mobcap with a pink bow while the other has her hair piled on top of her head. They both have dark brown brows, blue painted eyes with black lid lines and pupils, and light coral lips. The bisque and modeling are sharp and this flipper is incised "8855" underneath.

Illustration FP19 is collectible not only due to her fine quality, but also because she carries her manufacturer's mark. She is incised under her skirt "8293" over the crossedhatched "G" of Carl Schneider, Erben, followed by "DEP" (this stands for "dépose" and indicates that an original model or photograph of the object had been depos-

ited at the local District Court in order to obtain protection against infringement of the design). Schneider registered this trademark in 1894, and another clue to the figurine's age is the molded cigarette held in her right hand (and seemingly in danger of setting afire her blonde hair adorned with pink and reddish plumes). The use of tobacco by women was not really accepted until the 1920s, and prior to the period, portraying a woman with a cigarette indicated she was a lady of easy virtue. Her upper torso was molded separately and applied at the waist and left elbow, allowing her head and right arm to be separate from the rest of the figure. She has one stroke brown brows, black dot eyes and lid lines, and deep coral mouth. Her low cut green bodice is trimmed in molded white eyelet and gilt, and her light pink skirt edged in yellow is decorated with gold trim and raised gilt dots. Her ribbed stockings were left white and she has deep pink heeled slippers. Underneath, as seen in *Illustration FP20*, her open knickers expose her rosy bottom, the only area decorated on her underside. The bisque is sharp and the decoration good. She is 2½in (6cm) tall and 3¾in (10cm) wide.

Illustration FP7. 3in (8cm) tall bisque flipper. Unmarked.

Illustration FP8. Underside of *Illustration FP7*.

Illustration FP10. Underside of *Illustration FP9.*

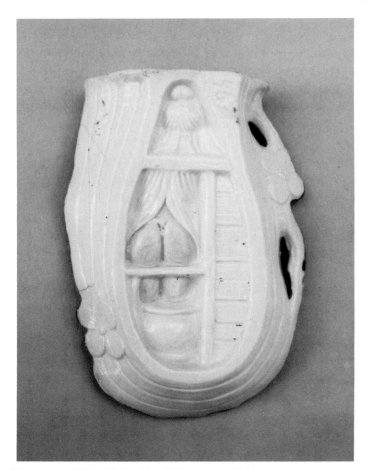

Illustration FP11. 4¾in (12cm) long china flipper. Incised "46" underneath.

Illustration FP12. Underside of *Illustration FP11*.

Illustration FP13. 5½in (17cm) tall bisque flipper. Caption reads "Oh! You pretty Gibson girl!". Unmarked.

Illustration FP14. Underside of *Illustration FP13*.

Illustration FP15. 5½in (17cm) tall bisque flipper. Unmarked.

Illustration FP16. Underside of *Illustration FP15*.

Illustration FP17. 5½in (17cm) wide bisque flipper. Incised "8855" underneath.

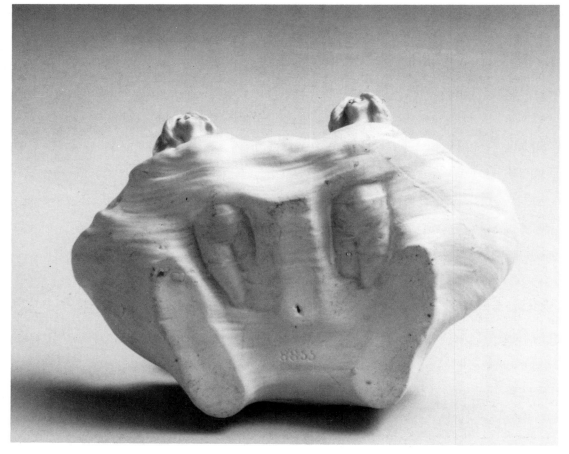

Illustration FP18. Underside of *Illustration FP17*.

Illustration FP19. 2½in (6cm) tall and 3¾in (10cm) wide bisque flipper made by Carl Schneider, Erben. Incised "8298//⚸ DEP" underneath. *Private Collection.*

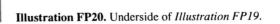

Illustration FP20. Underside of *Illustration FP19.*

End of an Era

Japan entered the bisque and china doll market relatively late. While traditional Japanese dolls had some popularity with children in Europe and the United States, Japan really did not make any great attempt to copy European methods of doll making until World War I. With German production and imports disrupted or curtailed, the Japanese moved into the market, in most cases either blatantly copying German dolls or even taking molds from German models. The Japanese showed little respect for copyrights, often either pirating a unique design, or only slightly modifying it. This applies to bathing beauties, nudies, and naughties as well as to dolls. Surprisingly, for a land renowned for its exquisite handicrafts and art, the Japanese products are almost without exception far inferior to the German models, from coarse bisque to sloppy decoration. The Japanese cut not just quality, but also price. After gaining their foothold in the market during the war, the Japanese manufacturers would remain serious competitors. Their cruder, but cheaper, products were yet another blow to a German industry trying to recover from a devastating war. Although Germany was capable of producing products of the highest quality through the early thirties, the flood of poor quality Japanese products into a market that once belonged only to Germany, the loss of skilled workers to the war, and the cost of rebuilding, forced many German makers to try penny pinching measures of their own, such as precolored bisque and not firing painted features. Although it is not correct to blame the Japanese for destroying the market for bathing beauties and their kin by dumping thousands of cheap, inferior versions, this activity did help speed the death of a fad that was probably already fading. Japanese products are still very common, and their poor quality repels serious collectors. However, they are a part of the history of naughties, nudies, and bathing beauties, and that is the reason for this chapter.

Illustration EE1 is typical of the open and notorious pirating the Japanese engaged in. 2½in (6cm) tall, she is undoubtedly a copy of *Illustration AP1*, shown in the Alfred Pensky section of "Ladies With A Past." Gone are the vivacious expression and realistic dimpled anatomy of the original. The face now is bland and flattened, the body dumpy and flaccid, and the once striking slim legs shapeless and sagging. Either the Japanese maker made a poor mold of the original, or had an unskilled artisan copy it. Marked on her back "Made in Japan," she wears a rusty red bathing cap, her dirty blonde bob hanging out at the sides. The one stroke brows are slightly darker blonde and her faded black dot eyes have heavy black lid lines. Her left arm was molded to her side to simplify production, although her legs were applied. Her one strap slippers match her cap. The bisque is rough and pitted and the complexion coat so poor she is piebald, varying from a unhealthy orangy tone to stark white.

Yet another design theft, *Illustration EE2* is no doubt a copy of *Illustration S13* of "Little Squirts." She appears to have been molded directly from a German piece. The fine windblown curls of the German original have degenerated to knobs and the hair is a thin wash of dirty yellow. The one stroke yellow brows have almost worn completely away, the entire eye socket was painted light blue, with black lid lines and pupils, and the lips are a harsh "V" of red. Her complexion coat is a splotchy faint pinkish wash and her chemise is tinted bright yellow only along the upper edge. Only one breast is pierced. The bisque is poor quality and badly finished and the unfired colors will wash away with a good scrubbing. 3in (8cm) tall, she is faintly stamped "MADE IN JAPAN" on her base, but even if she was not marked, her inferior workmanship would indicate her country of origin was Japan, not Germany.

Illustration EE3 is unmarked, but like *Illustration EE2*, his crude decoration and poor bisque indicate he is of Japanese production. A pirated version of *Illustration S4 and S5* of "Little Squirts," he stands 3½in (9cm) tall. His stocking cap is an uneven red brown and his yellow hair has no curls. The one stroke brows and lid lines are dark brown and the eyes a glossy deep blue. His mouth is made of two tiny dabs of dark shiny red. The nightshirt is a faint wash of blue, and, other than his unevenly blushed cheeks, he has no skin tone. The inferior bisque has a chalky feel and he is very light for his size.

Illustration EE4 is of even poorer workmanship. 4in (10cm) tall, including his original rubber cap, he is poorly modeled, looking clumsy and flattened. His hair is indicated only by dents in his scalp, faintly airbrushed black, his eyes are only black pupils dabbed in the middle of white irises, and the mouth is simply a red dribble. Of dark brown painted bisque, he lacks the coy naughtiness of the little German boys, and in fact, has no real appeal at all. "JAPAN" is incised between his shoulder blades.

Stamped underneath in deep orange "MADE IN OCCU-PIED JAPAN," *Illustration EE5* demonstrates just how late naughties were made (the German piece he was copied from was produced over a decade earlier). 2½in (9cm) long, this china dog is most unquestionably a male. His spots are brown, his goggle eyes black circles with upglancing pupils, and his collar and frowning mouth the same color as the stamp on his belly. The opening for water is the tip of his tail, and it squirts from under his upraised left leg. There are people who collect the products from occupied Japan, so this little dog would probably appeal to them as much as to a collector of naughties.

Illustration EE6 also is copied from a German original, but her quality is quite good and, if she were not incised "MADE IN JAPAN" across her upper back, she might pass for a late, adequate German piece. The German original appears as both a mohair wigged bather with ballet type slippers or as a molded hair, barefoot version. In this Japanese copy, her molded bob is an orangy dark blonde and the one stroke brows a shade darker. The painted blue eyes have black pupils and lid lines, as well as bright pink eyeshadow. The nose dots and full lips are deep red and there is a slight dimple painted in her chin. Although her cheeks are so heavily blushed she looks feverish, overall the facial decoration is acceptable. Her figure is quite nicely proportioned and the bisque sharp with a slight oily sheen. She at first appears to have stark white skin, but a flesh tone blotch across the back of her thighs and buttocks and fainter spots on her back and sides indicate a half-hearted attempt to complexion coat her. Her head and neck were applied,

and she is a nice size at 6½in (17cm) long. Overall, she shows that the Japanese were capable of decent workmanship and if even this standard had been maintained, their adverse impact on the market might not have been so severe. However, even this merely acceptable quality is the exception, rather than the rule.

Illustration EE7 also shows that the Japanese could produce an adequate piece when they tried. In fact, in many ways she is superior to the German turtle lady in *Illustration M9* of "Mermaids and Sea Nymphs," as she has a more elaborate hairstyle, openings between her arms and torso, and a more detailed face. 5½in (14cm) long, her towering hair is glossy black. Her one stroke brows are brown and her black dot eyes have red and black lid lines. The nose dots are light coral and her mouth dark red. For all the detail, the painting is rather sloppy, and her cheeks have an unattractive orange blush. Although the head and arms were molded separately and applied, the application lines were not finished and a piece of mold debris is stuck under her chin. The turtle shell, done in shades of tan and decorated even underneath, is very well modeled. The incised "MADE IN JAPAN" is so cleverly worked into the detailed plates

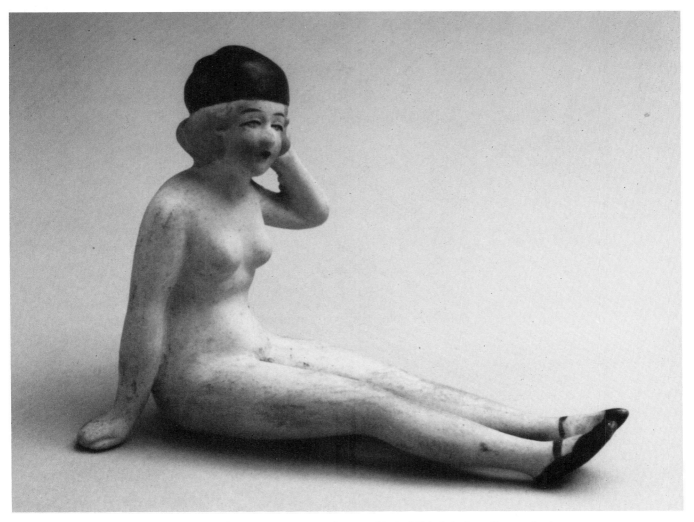

Illustration EE1. 2½in (6cm) tall bisque figurine. Marked "Made in Japan" across back.

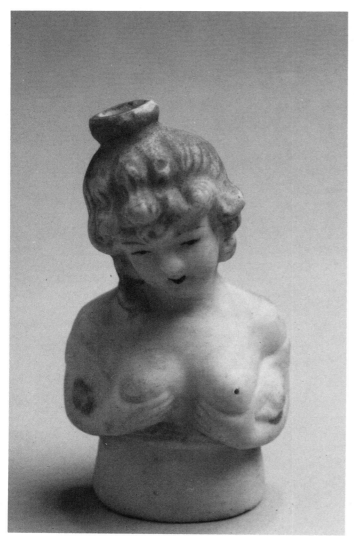

(Above)
Illustration EE2. 3in (8cm) tall bisque squirter. Stamped "MADE IN JAPAN" on base

(Right)
Illustration EE3. 3½in (9cm) tall bisque squirter. No marks.

underneath, it takes some time to find it. Her black stockinged ankles and black slippers peek out from behind. Inside, shown in *Illustration EE8*, only her pink bottom, exposed by her opened split knickers (certainly an anachronism at the time she was produced), is tinted. The bisque is very good for a Japanese piece and overall she meets, and even beats, many German works of the same genre. Even for a collector who usually scorns Japanese pieces, she would be a nice addition to a collection, provided the price was right, meaning low.

Although unmarked, my suspicion is that *Illustration EE9* is Japanese, despite her good bisque and workmanship. 5in (13cm) long, she wears her original "grass skirt." She appears to have been copied from a version of *Illustration AP4*, shown in the Alfred Pensky section of "Ladies With A Past". Her black wavy hair has sharply delineated curls and

the headband is a deep orange dotted with gold, a color more often favored by the Japanese than the Germans. Her facial features are very sharp and clear, as if after she was removed from the mold someone skillfully went over them with a sharp sculpting tool. Her eyes, under rather beetling brows, have white irises and black pupils and the lips are decorated only by a line of orange between. Although her arms and shoulders are rather heavy, her hips and waist are slim and her legs long and lithe. The painted complexion coat is rather even and at first could pass as fired, except for the tiny chips at the feet and a small flake on the right buttock. The underlying bisque appears to be smooth, sharp, and well finished. However, while she could pass for late German piece, I have seen a seated black lady with the same headband marked as Japanese. Black ladies of good quality are so scarce, however, they are collectible, whether German or Japanese.

Illustration EE4. 4in (10cm) tall painted bisque squirter. Incised "Japan".

Illustration EE5. 2½in (9cm) long china squirter. Stamped "MADE IN OCCUPIED JAPAN" in orange on stomach.

Illustration EE6. 6½in (17cm) long bisque figurine. Incised "MADE IN JAPAN" across upper back.

(Above)
Illustration EE7. 5½in (14cm) long bisque turtle lady. Incised "MADE IN JAPAN" on bottom of turtle shell.

(Right)
Illustration EE8. Interior view of *Illustration EE7*.

Illustration EE9. 5in (13cm) long painted bisque figurine, wearing original "grass skirt." Unmarked.

Parting Notes

One of the first questions always asked of a collector is, "Where do you find all these things?" For a collector of naughties, nudies, and bathing beauties, the response is "everywhere" (and sometimes, it seems, nowhere). Like their sisters, the half dolls, they sometimes turn up at an antique doll show or shop. Antique shows, stores, and malls are also to be searched. In my experience, hunting through the proliferating flea markets and garage and estate sales has not been particularly productive. In fact, I no longer even bother attending these latter events, unless I know there will be a sizable turnout of antique dealers or if it is an estate sale that will include a large number of antiques. This is not to suggest that a lucky collector might not stumble on a treasure at a weekend swap meet or among the jumbled junk of a garage sale, but most of us have only so much time we can spend looking for new ladies and must attend to such mundane matters as earning a living and maintaining a household. Unless a collector is independently wealthy in time as well as resources, he or she has only limited hours to spend searching and should focus on those places where the chance of success is more substantial. At a show or shop, do not just simply glance into the displays of figurines. Many times a dealer may only have a single such item and will tuck it into a small glass case among other tiny treasures, use it to drape jewelry or lace over for display, or just stick it anywhere there is a space. If a dealer has several pieces of the type and quality you seek, but they are all duplicates of items in your collection, do not be shy about asking if he or she has any others. Remember, a dealer cannot bring everything to a show or have had time to display everything in the shop. Even if he or she does not, the dealer may know of another who carries such items or be about to purchase a collection. If you have a business card, print legibly what items you are interested in on the back, and give it to the dealer with the polite request he or she contact you if the dealer runs into more such items (if you do not have a business card, I recommend the minor investment of having some printed with your name, address, telephone number, and what you collect); if you do find something to your taste and make a purchase, be sure to give the dealer this information. Most dealers keep a record of their past customers and their wants, but it never hurts to reinforce you desires. You may be surprised to suddenly receive a letter offering some treasure many months after you left the show or shop. While dealers love antiques, they are also in business, and if they see something they think is in a customer's taste and price range they will often purchase it since they have a certain sale and profit.

However, bathing beauties and their kin can be fickle, and one can search dozens of shows and shops without the slightest success. The old motto, "It never hurts to advertise," is as applicable to a collector as to a business. Throughout the country there are a number of weekly or monthly antique publications that carry want ads where a collector can list his or her interests, and there are also several "want books," updated annually, that offer the same services. The cost is usually minimal (and sometimes free), but can put you in contact with dealers and fellow collectors all over the country. However, be very specific as to your wants. If you do not want Japanese items, or you do not like china pieces, be sure to so state. Most of these publications have set categories for ads, and I have found my most productive ads have appeared under "Dolls Wanted" or "Miscellaneous Wanted." Also, this is a good way to meet fellow collectors and it is always fun to correspond with others, swapping information or stories of the latest finds.

Such ads often bring in responses, sometimes months after the ad first appeared. The best are accompanied by a clear description and photograph, but many times the letter contains nothing more than a size and vague description (i.e.: I have a bathing beauty, about 3 inches long, in striped suit for $75). Since many of these correspondents are not collectors or dealers, they do not understand the importance of position, workmanship, and condition. You will need to contact the writer and politely interrogate him or her for the important information you need. Be patient, since many people use the term china for bisque and do not understand the difference between precolored and tinted bisque, you may have to do a little long distance educating. If you do decide to purchase, mail order requires a certain amount of trust in your fellow man or woman. The tradition is not to ship the goods until the money has been received. However, in all my years of collecting, I have yet to have a seller take my money and not send me my purchase. Ask the seller what his or her return privilege policy is (usually you will have three to five days to return the item for a refund for any reason you are not satisfied) and if the price includes postage and insurance. If postage and insurance are not included, ask the seller what he or she estimates the cost will be, and add that to the price (insist on insurance, since you are dealing with an antique, fragile figurine). Usually, if you pay by check, the item will not be shipped until the check has cleared, but if you send a money order or cashier's check, the item is shipped upon receipt. Send a cover letter setting out in detail the item you are purchasing, the amount of the item and, if applicable, postage and insurance, confirming the return privilege, and giving any instructions where the package should be sent. If you do have any problems, the letter may be an important piece of evidence.

Auctions are another source, especially auctions of antique dolls. Many ads for auctions appear in periodicals aimed towards antiquers, and often list or picture items that will be sold. Legitimate auctions also have a preview period that allows potential purchasers to peruse the items prior to the auction. There are a number of companies that specialize in doll auctions and produce beautiful, detailed catalogues, as well as allow absentee bidding. They are more then happy to put you on their mailing lists for flyers announcing each auction and briefly describing the collections to be sold. The rules differ for each company, and you will need to determine how absentee bids are made, what guarantees each company gives as to descriptions in their catalogues, what the return policy is if an item is not as described, and whether there is a buyer's premium. If you have any antique doll collecting friends, you may want to talk to them as to which of these companies they have dealt with and might recommend. As catalogues can be rather expensive, if the flyer does not describe or picture bathing beauties or their kin, prior to ordering a catalogue, I recommend calling the company, explaining that you only collect these particular items, and asking if there will be anything that might be of

interest to you at the auction. I have never had a problem getting a courteous and helpful reply. Auction prices are often unpredictable, since they depend so much on who is present and how badly the buyer wants an item. However, luck may be with you and you can purchase a prize for a pittance. Even if you are not fortunate enough to make the winning bid, such catalogues are often excellent educational material (and wonderful "wish books"), giving the collector a chance to become acquainted with different items, marks, and makers.

Once you have found a possible treasure, what should you look for? The quality of the bisque and decoration, as well as the condition of the piece, are of utmost importance. In tinted bisque, the bisque should be smooth, the color evenly applied, and the features well painted. For precolored bisque pieces, the best bisque is an even pale pink without the unattractive greasy sheen and the features should be nicely painted and not worn away or faded. Generally, a tinted bisque piece is more desirable, since the complexion coat had to be padded on, an extra step requiring great skill, but there are excellent precolored pieces, as well as very poor tinted bisque items. A precolored bisque piece in an unusual pose certainly would be more collectible than a simple tinted bisque piece with poorly done complexion and features, but when confronted with similar tinted and

Illustration PN1. View of miniature bordello using two Alfred Pensky nudies and other tiny antiques.

precolored bisque pieces at around the same price, in most cases the tinted bisque items will be more collectible.

The collector must remember that, as hard as they may be to find today, naughties, nudies, and bathing beauties were mass produced, hand done, and usually fairly inexpensive, novelties produced in factories without modern equipment and conveniences. A collector cannot expect absolute perfection. The German manufacturers were in business, and they had no qualms about marketing a piece with small imperfections if it still would coax pennies from some consumer's pocket. Minor, inconspicuous factory flaws, such as a faint kiln line under the arm, one eyebrow ever so slightly higher than the other, or a bit of tiny slag on the torso, do not seriously detract from the figurine's value or desirability. However, a major or obvious flaw, such as a bubble at the end of a nose or a poorly applied complexion coat, adversely affects a piece's collectibility, and should be reflected in the price. Only perfect pieces can command the highest prices.

Damage and wear also must be taken into account when puzzling about a potential purchase. Whether a collector should even consider buying a damaged piece depends on the rarity of the item, the extent of the damage, and, of course, the price. The common, later precolored bisque or china pieces should be perfect for purchase, unless the price is very cheap. For better or less common items, very minor damage, such as a tiny flake off a toe or a finger tip or a slight small rub in the complexion coat, does not really distract from collectibility, although the damage should be reflected somewhat in the price. More serious damage, such as a limb that has been broken and reglued, is really acceptable only in the finest of bathing beauties or ladies, and then only if the price is significantly lower than for a perfect piece. For example, a common precolored bisque bathing beauty that has had her legs snapped off and reglued is really not worth purchasing, unless the price is very low. However, a fine quality wigged bather in the remains of her original swimsuit with an arm that has been broken off and cleanly reglued is worth considering, if the seller has considered the damage in the price. Missing fingers or toes are also really only acceptable if the piece is very fine, and the price has been substantially lowered to take the damage into account. If a hand, foot, or limb is missing, unless the piece is of the highest quality, and the price is the lowest, the figurine is best passed over by the collector. Never purchase a piece on the grounds that it can be restored. Many restorers are not capable of properly repairing such delicate pieces. Too often I have seen "professionally restored" pieces with clumsy replaced limbs and overpainting that extends far beyond the broken area (on one piece I saw, the restorer, in repairing a simple clean break on one arm, airbrushed both arms from wrist to shoulder with a heavy coat of paint so they would "match"). Professional restorers skilled enough to acceptably restore pieces without sanding or extensive overpainting are hard to find and generally expensive. There is nothing wrong with a collector buying a broken, but good, piece with the idea he or she will keep it until he or she stumbles upon a perfect version, but the collector should not pay near top price for a damaged figurine on the grounds that it can be "restored". Even the best restoration is visible to the alert collector. On bisque pieces, the material used to make new fingers, toes, or limbs lacks the flaky, porous feel of the old bisque and often the new part does not match the delicacy and symmetry of the rest of the piece. To cover breaks or match new parts, the damage, and the surrounding bisque, must be overpainted. It is nearly impossible to perfectly match the color of the original bisque, and as the paint, whether brush applied or airbrushed, will fill up the pores in the bisque, the painted areas will have a denser, smoother appearance and feel. Repairs on china can be harder to detect, as a glaze-like substance is painted over the restoration, but careful examination will usually detect a difference in color, texture, or a part that does not quite blend in. A small jeweler's loop carried in purse or pocket is a highly recommended tool. Examining and handling pieces, both perfect and restored, will help sharpen the collector's eye until he or she can instantly spot a repair. A repaired piece is like a broken piece, and whether it should even be considered for purchase depends on the desirability of the figurine itself, the extent and quality of the repair, and how the restoration is reflected in the price.

The desirability of a piece also depends on its rarity and quality. In many ways, bathing beauties, naughties, and nudies can be judged somewhat like pincushion dolls. The most common are made in a simple two part mold with no opening between the body and the limbs or between the limbs. The next step up may have an opening between one or both arms and the body, or between the legs, but the arms still return to the body and the legs are still joined. The finest have free limbs, such as an arm that extends completely away from the body or a leg that crosses, but is not joined to, its fellow. The more complicated the pose, the more complex the mold, the more skill required in the completion, and, consequently, the more desirable the figurine. The fine wigged ladies required more work and expense initially, and this is reflected in their price even today. Among the wigged bathing beauties and their kin: molded together pairs; bathing beauties that do more than simply look pretty, such as reading a book, petting a kitten, or playing a mandolin; male bathers (since they cannot really be called "beauties," perhaps they can be referred to as "beach boys"); or, variations on the theme, such as ethnic ladies or plump matrons are the hardest to find, and command the highest prices. Black stockings and molded underwear are always desirable, provided the piece is well done and of good quality. Among squirters, ladies, particularly those that squirt between their legs, are far less common than cute little boys, and for flippers, the quality of the work and the humor of the theme are important concerns. Much, of course, depends on the collector's taste, and no buy is a bargain if the collector really does not care for the piece (although duplicates are always nice for sale or trade, a collector must remember that he or she could still be "stuck" with the piece for quite a while).

Reproductions do not yet seem to be a problem in this area of collecting. The most common figurines do not command enough of a price to make them worth reproducing, and the best pieces would be so costly to reproduce that a new piece would almost have to sell at the same price as the antique. This is not to say that someday someone might not try his or her hand at reproduction. First, a mold would have to be made, and the more desirable pieces most worth reproducing would require a skilled mold maker, and probably multiple molds (that would have to be replaced every fifty castings or so). Modern bisque has a completely different feel from the old; the new slip is so well compounded, and modern equipment so good, that it produces an almost slippery smooth bisque, while even the best old bisque has a porous "drag" to it (most modern artists also tend to use precolored slip, few being skilled enough to pad on an acceptable complexion coat). Although the German factory workers toiled long hours in factories without mod-

ern lighting, proper ventilation, or air conditioning, often in conditions that endangered their health, for paltry paychecks, the work they did is difficult for all but the best modern doll artist to reproduce. A collector who tries copying those tiny features quickly learns how difficult it is to paint matching eyebrows or daintily bow a lip even with the best equipment. Duplicating the look and feel of the old bisque, as well as the delicate decoration, would require a very talented artist, and it is unlikely one so skilled would sell such work cheap enough to make it worth his or her while to pass the new off as old. China pieces are more forgiving for the reproduction artist, as the glaze can disguise the feel of new slip and soften the features, but as the even finest china pieces do not seem to claim the price of the bisque, again it is not yet worth someone's while to reproduce figurines good enough to try to pass off as antiques. One of the best protections against reproductions, and repairs, is to have the seller write a full description of the

Illustration PN2. Display of wigged bathing beauties using an old print as a background and cat litter as "sand."

item, including that it is old and detailing the condition, on the sales receipt. If later the item is found to be not as represented, the buyer can use the receipt as a warranty and demand a refund.

Once a lucky collector has purchased a treasure, he or she should have a method for saving receipts and documenting his or her collection. A card file with an index card fully describing each piece, the date purchased, and the purchase price, with a photograph attached, is the most manual method. A more technically adept collector can use his or her personal computer to record and store such information or make a video record, filming each item while describing it. Whichever method is used, it is a good idea to have a copy tucked away in a different location (i.e.: one at home and the other at the office or in a safe deposit box). A fine or extensive collection should be insured; there are special policies available for antiques and members of the United Federation of Doll Clubs can obtain a policy that covers antique dolls and doll related items.

Of course, collecting is no fun unless your finds can be displayed. Glass fronted display cases are the best, although open shelves, shadow boxes, and table tops are fine if the figurine is safe from falls. Much of my collection is displayed in my guest bathroom, making it more popular with visitors than most powder rooms warrant. As most of these figurines display a touch of whimsy or humor, this can be carried over to their display. *Illustration PN1* shows a miniature bordello used to display two of my Alfred Pensky figurines, as well as many other antique miniatures. *Illustration PN2* demonstrates a display using an old calendar print of a seashore for the background and some fine grained cat litter as "sand."

Whether displayed behind glass doors or in the open, the figurine is safest secured to the surface. Most stores that sell stationary supplies carry a putty like substance, which is marketed under various names, that is used to stick posters and pictures on walls and perform other such tasks. The putty is removable, reusable, and does not discolor bisque or china (although it should not be used on cloth). A small ball of such putty discretely tucked under a supporting elbow, knee, or tummy, will keep the knick-knack from being bumped over by a careless guest, a gust of wind, or a slamming door. Dusting your collection, even if kept behind glass, is important, and by securing your collectibles, they can be safely dusted with a light touch and a feather duster.

The final question is how much should one pay, and my answer is pay what you can afford and feel is fair. Pricing is a tricky matter, especially in this area of collecting. A price that will cause a figurine to be snapped up on the East or West coasts may leave the same piece sitting on the shelf in the Midwest. Also, a piece's appeal can affect the price. If someone just has to have a certain item, and has the money to fulfill his or her desire, the price can skyrocket; on the other hand, an excellent piece can go begging because it just did not catch anyone's eye. At one auction, for example, an admittedly very lovely all original wigged bathing beauty went for well over two thousand dollars. Yet, shortly afterwards, the same model, also all original, went for under a third of the previous price at another auction. In another auction, a large, but rather common, Alfred Pensky precolored nudie went for hundreds of dollars, while, in that same auction, a lot of three bathing beauties that included a wigged, albeit tiny, lady and a fine tinted bisque bather in a lovely striped suit and unusual pose (and a probable Goebel to boot!), went for under three hundred dollars. The fine quality wigged bathing beauties are popular right now and currently commanding premium prices of several hundred dollars each, but there are bargains out there. Many of the nudies, naughties, flippers, and squirters can be found at very reasonable prices. A charming and enjoyable collection can be put together on a budget, with a little persistence, education, and luck. Unfortunately, there seems to be a craze to treat collecting as an investment, not a pleasurable pasttime, and a figurine's price becomes its most important feature. Anyone with enough money can go out and buy a collection, but for the true collector the challenge of the hunt, the uncovering of a treasure, and the piecing together of scattered clues to try to solve the mystery of who made each prized piece, when, and where is as enjoyable as the actual accumulation of a collection. And, after all, if collecting is not fun, why bother?

Bibliography

Black, J. Anderson and Garland, Madge, *A History of Fashion* (William Morrow and Company, Inc., New York 1975)

Bowman, Sara and Molinare, Micheal, *A Fashion for Extravagence— Art Deco Fabrics and Fashions* (E.P. Dutton, New York 1985)

Cieslik, Jurgen and Marianne, **German Doll Encyclopedia** (Hobby House Press, Inc., Maryland 1985)

Coleman, Dorothy S., Elizabeth A., and Evelyn J., *The Collector's Encyclopedia of Dolls, Volume II* (Crown Publisher, Inc., New York 1986)

Colette, *The Collected Stories of Colette*, edit. Robert Phelps (Farrar Straus Giroux, New York 1984)

Croutier, Alev Lytle, *Harem — The World Behind the Veil* (Abbeville Press, New York 1989)

Dorman, Genevieve, *Colette — A Passion for Life* (Abbeville Press, New York 1985)

Edwig, Elizabeth, *Dress and Undress — A History of Women's Underwear* (Drama Book Specialists 1978)

Edwig, Elizabeth, *History of Twentieth Century Fashion* (Barnes and Noble 1985)

Farrah, Ibrahim, "Photos Please" in *Arabesque*, Volume XIII, No. IV, November-December 1987

Hammond, Paul, *French Undressing — Naughty Postcards from 1900 to 1920* (Bloomsbury Books, London 1988)

Hughes-Hallett, *Cleopatra — Histories, Dreams, and Distortions* (Harper and Row, New York 1990)

Kidwell, Caludia Brush and Steele, Valerie, *Men and Women* (Smithsonian Institute Press 1989)

Kirsch, Francine, "The Fanciest of Printed Fabrics" in *The Antique Trader Weekly*, Volume 34, issue 13, March 28, 1990

Knapp, Bettina L., "Dance Archeology: Orientalia — Salome Mania" in *Arabesque*, Volume XIII, No. IV, November-December 1987

Marion, Friede and Werner, Norma, *The Collector's Encyclopedia of Half Dolls* (Crown Publishers, Inc., New York 1979)

Mulvagh, Jane, *Vogue; A History of Twentieth Century Fashion* (Viking 1988)

Ostrovsky, Erika, *Eye of Dawn — The Rise and Fall of Mata Hari* (Dorset Press, New York 1989)

Rollasan, Jane, *The Complete Manual of Airbrushing* (Alfred A. Knopf, New York 1991)

Steele, Valerie, *Fashion and Eroticism* (Oxford University Press 1985)

Values Guide

A values guide is just that, a guide. Values, especially for collectibles as varied and diverse as these, cannot be set in stone. A bargain in one area of the country may go begging for buyers in another. A lovely lady may remain lonely on an antique shop shelf simply because she has not engaged any browser's fancy. Another may go for many times her expected price because some collector compulsively coveted her. This is why I have tried to come up with a reasonable range. I am a collector, not a dealer, and although I try to track prices through auction catalogues and antiques periodicals, I cannot claim to have canvassed antique shops throughout the country. The following prices are good faith estimates based on my personal experience. Please treat them as well meant advice, not as absolutes.

The prices are based on figurines in good condition with no damage, of fine quality bisque or china (for the type), and nice decoration. Noticeable factory flaws, chips, rubs, worn or washed away features, or other damage will lower the price. Wigged bathing beauties and ladies should have original or suitable old wigs. Such items with their original suits in good to mint condition will command the highest prices. These are retail prices, such as you might see in a shop. A collector, without the worry of store rent and overhead, selling privately to a fellow collector or to a dealer cannot expect as high a price.

Page #	Illustration #	Value	Page #	Illustration #	Value	Page #	Illustration #	Value
Crowning Glory			36	M3	$175 - $225	**One Thousand and One Nights**		
18	CG1	$1500 - $2000	37	M4	$250 - $300	56	H1	$175 - $225
19	CG2	$800 - $1000		M5	$125 - $175		H2	$200 - $250
22	CG4	$525 - $725	38	M6	$250 - $300	57	H3	$500 - $700
	CG6	$600 - $800	39	M8	$200 - $250		H5	$325 - $375
23	CG8	$450 - $650	40	M9	$150 - $200	**Ladies with a Past**		
	CG10	$425 - $625	**Naughty, but Nice**			**Dressel, Kister and Company**		
	CG11	$400 - $600	42	NN1	$550 - $750	60	DK1	$200 - $250
24	CG12	$500 - $700	43	NN2	$250 - $300		DK2	$225 - $275
	CG13	$800 - $1000		NN3	$250 - $300	**Galluba and Hofmann**		
25	CG16	$700 - $900	45	NN4	$300 - $350	61	GH1	$550 - $750
	CG18	$600 - $800		NN6	$225 - $275		GH2	$250 - $300
26	CG19	$700 - $900	46	NN7	$300 - $350	63	GH4	$450 - $500
	CG20	$650 - $850		NN8	$225 - $275	64	GH5	$800 - $1000
27	CG21	$400 - $600		NN9	$125 - $175	65	GH7	$625 - $825
	CG22	$400 - $600	47	NN10	$125 - $175	66	GH8	$450 - $650
By the Sea				NN11	$300 - $350		GH9	$200 - $250
29	BS1	$145 - $195		NN12	$225 - $275	**William Goebel**		
30	BS2	$300 - $350	**Working Girls**			67	G1	$350 - $400
31	BS3	$110 - $160	49	WG1	$175 - $225	68	G3	$350 - $400
	BS4	$175 - $225		WG2	$125 - $175	69	G4	$250 - $300
32	BS5	$175 - $225	50	WG3	$125 - $175		G5	$250 - $300
	BS6	$125 - $175	51	WG4	$400 - $450		G6	$200 - $250
33	BS7	$125 - $175		WG5	$150 - $200	70	G7	$300 - $350
	BS8	$ 65 - $115		WG6	$200 - $250		G8	$250 - $300
	BS9	$ 65 - $115	52	WG7	$125 - $175	71	G10	$400 - $450
34	BS10	$250 - $300	53	WG8	$100 - $150	72	G11	$800 - $1000
	BS11	$175 - $225		WG9	$125 - $175		G12	$150 - $200
	BS12	$175 - $225	54	WG10	$275 - $325	**Alfred Pensky**		
Mermaids and Sea Nymphs				WG12	$ 50 - $100	73	AP1	$125 - $175
35	M1	$100 - $150				74	AP2	$200 - $250
	M2	$150 - $200				75	AP3	$ 65 - $ 90

Page #	Illustration #	Value	Page #	Illustration #	Value	Page #	Illustration #	Value
76	AP4	$ 65 - $ 90	86	S8	$130 - $180	94	FP7	$250 - $300
	AP5	$125 - $175	87	S9	$175 - $225	95	FP9	$175 - $200
Schafer and Vater				S10	$130 - $180	96	FP11	$125 - $150
77	SV1	$175 - $225	88	S11	$195 - $225		FP13	$250 - $300
79	SV2	$175 - $225		S12	$185 - $210	97	FP15	$200 - $250
80	SV4	$325 - $375		S13	$175 - $200	98	FP17	$225 - $275
	SV5	$300 - $350		S14	$175 - $200	99	FP19	$250 - $300
	SV6	$300 - $350	89	S15	$185 - $210	**End of an Era**		
81	SV7	$325 - $375		S16	$175 - $200	101	EE1	$ 35 - $ 60
	SV8	$200 - $250		S17	$175 - $200	102	EE2	$ 25 - $ 50
	SV9	$200 - $250	90	S18	$185 - $210		EE3	$ 25 - $ 50
	SV10	$350 - $400		S19	$185 - $200	103	EE4	$ 25 - $ 50
Little Squirts				S20	$165 - $190		EE5	$ 45 - $ 65
82	S1	$ 65 - $115		S21	$165 - $190		EE6	$125 - $175
84	S2	$125 - $175	**The Flip Side**			104	EE7	$ 50 - $100
	S3	$125 - $175	92	FP1	$185 - $210		EE9	$175 - $200
85	S4	$100 - $150		FP3	$250 - $300			
	S5	$ 95 - $145	93	FP5	$225 - $275			
	S6	$130 - $180						
	S7	$150 - $200						

Photograph by Kaye Marvins Studio, Houston, Texas

ABOUT THE AUTHOR

The author's interest in antique dolls began at the age of eleven, when an aunt gave her a china doll head. Another gift started her collection of naughties, nudies, and bathing beauties. Twenty years ago, her mother purchased a squirter of a boy on a chamberpot in Berkeley, California and sent it to the author, who was in her first year of college at the University of Texas at Austin. Intrigued by the little figurine, the author began to search out similar items. Unfortunately, the available reference material on these odd collectibles was sparse, and she began to collect information as well as new naughties. Her interest in women's history also spurred her collection of bathing beauties and their sisters, as in their own way they represent the changes in society, and its attitude toward women, that took place during the first three decades of this century.

The author has previously published an article on Goebel bathing beauties in *Doll Reader®* magazine. A member of the United Federation of Doll Clubs, she currently lives in Austin, Texas, where she works as an attorney. She also collects all-bisque and miniature dolls.